A COMPANION BOOK TO "THE AWAKENING TETRALOGY"

D0993053

Spiritual Reflections

A BOOK ABOUT AWAKENING AND ENLIGHTENMENT

BY KEN LUBALL AND BODHI ("A SPIRIT GUIDE")

Author's Note:

"Spiritual Reflections: A Book About Awakening and Enlightenment" is a book of poetry, consisting of 200 free verse Spiritual poems. These poems include the reflections seen in the four spiritual novels in *"The Awakening Tetralogy"*, in addition to many others not yet published. The underlying theme of these poems is Spirituality, each illustrating different aspects of Awakening and Enlightenment. To truly understand each reflection, read only 2 or 3 a day and "reflect".

Spirituality is the belief there is a piece of God (a Spirit or Soul) within every life and, because of this, each life is Important, Equal, and Connected.

My goal writing the four books in *The Awakening Tetralogy* and this book of Spiritually inspired poetry, was to try to *Awaken* and help others, who are *Awakened*, more fully understand what *Enlightenment* is, so their Journey Through Life may be more fully realized.

Bodhi is my *"Spirit Guide";* he is able to easily communicate with me as I write down his thoughts. Though my journey towards

Enlightenment is not yet complete, *Bodhi,* being a *Spirit Guide,* most certainly is *Enlightened.* We wrote this book of Spiritual Reflections together for all those seeking to begin the *Awakening* process *or* who have *Awoken* and seek to venture further on their path towards *Enlightenment.* Learn more about each of the Spiritual books in *"The Awakening Tetralogy"* at my website:

http://kenluball.com

The Four books in *"The Awakening Tetralogy"* include:

Today I Am Going to Die: Choices in Life
The Spirit Guide: Journey Through Life
Tranquility: A Village of Hope
The Illusion of Happiness: Choosing Love Over Fear

The Butterfly

It is not others who must change (Ego).

It is you who must first evolve (Spirit).

Only then will you begin to come

Out of your cocoon and

Become a butterfly.

The Three Stages of Enlightenment

The First Stage of Enlightenment – Being Asleep

The first stage of Enlightenment begins when we are born,

As we are Socialized and Taught what to Believe (Ego),

As we are exposed to and Accept the mores of the society we are

born into.

With our birth, our identity is often already pre-determined.

The color of our skin, country we are born into, religion,

And many other man-made comparisons often dictate our future in

the world.

We Believe these comparisons are true by observing others,

Reading about them in books and newspapers and by watching TV

and movies.

Most people Believe and Internalize these differences, further

proving to themselves

They are better, more important than another.

Those who Accept and Believe what they were Taught is true,

Despite their Success in life, remain Asleep, destined to live a life of

mediocrity,

Believing their Happiness and Meaning will come from the World.

"It Will Not".

The Second Stage of Enlightenment – Awakening

Those who Awaken begin to question if everything we Learned and

Accepted

To be real in life, as we were growing up, was true.

A feeling begins to flourish within, no longer able to be ignored,

Questioning the validity of Everything we once Believed.

Though we may be leading a "successful" life, be wealthy, famous,

Or any other Learned comparison as to what success is,

It no longer quells the uneasy feelings we experience coming from

deep Within us.

The anguish we feel emanates from our Spirit, present Within every

life.

Some may call the Spirit God/Soul/Essence or assign it another name.

It does not matter.

It represents our Guide through life and gives our life Meaning.

We Awaken when we first sense something is wrong,

Begin to question if what we Learned and Accepted was true may Not have been,

Beginning us on a journey we have no choice but to pursue.

A Journey Towards Enlightenment.

The Third Stage of Enlightenment – Enlightenment

Enlightenment happens when we finally Accept

Everything we Learned and Believed to be true was Not.

Despite our Appearance, Wealth, Job, Material Possessions,

Or any other comparison we were Taught differentiates us from each other,

We now realize we are Not better or more important than anyone else.

We begin to Hear our Spirit within, embracing its message

By Sharing our Love unconditionally with all others.

Though what we Learned when we were young will remain with us

(Ego)

Its influence on our life is now minimal.

Instead of competing, we now wish to cooperate.

Instead of living in Fear, we now seek to live our life with Love.

And instead of desiring only what is Best for Ourselves,

We now wish to Selflessly help Others, to ease their Journey

Through Life.

With this change and Acceptance of the Spirit's message

We move further along the path towards Enlightenment.

With Awakening Everything Changes

It's all part of the journey.

Once you Awaken, the only certainty is your life

Will never be the same and there is no turning back.

Everything in your life will change, including your friendships, relationships

And patience for the games people play who remain asleep.

Awakening happens when you begin to question everything you Learned.

Enlightenment though will only happen when you truly

Accept everything you Learned in life was Untrue.

The truth has always been Within.

Listen Quietly for all the answers you seek.

The Play

On the day we are going to die when the Ego finally surrenders

Its hold on our life, we will understand our entire life was a Play.

It was all Make-Believe.

We acted our part so well we never knew it was not real.

Life is just an Illusion, where we all have our bit parts in the play.

If we follow the script, as we Learned to do as we are growing up,

The answers we seek about life may elude us.

It is only when we act outside the boundaries of the script and

Awake,

The answers we seek may finally reveal themselves.

The Matrix

The Matrix is a world where most are Asleep,

Living in a Learned Reality Accepted as the Truth.

Those who remain sleeping throughout their lives

Seek their Truth in the World, Believing what they were Taught

As they were growing up will bring them Meaning and Happiness.

"It Will Not".

When we first Awake we start to question if that belief is right.

Despite how "successful" our life has been, sensing a Voice we

begin to Hear Within,

The norms we once unquestionably Learned and Accepted as truth

No longer Make sense to us.

The Voice we hear tells us of Unconditional Love,

Hope, Equality, Helping Others, and all other Positive Caring values

Shared Selflessly with all others.

The Matrix we once understood and accepted as our reality

Begins to dissolve, leaving an unrecognizable world,

A world where Love (Spirit) becomes predominant over Fear (Ego).

Rather than compete against each other to survive in the world,

We desire to Help each other instead.

Living in such a world is possible.

To do so, Listen to the voice you Hear Within,

Open your Heart to the possibility's life offers,

Allowing your Matrix to melt away,

Revealing the true Purpose of Life in its wake.

The Suitcase

I would like you to picture an open suitcase.

Before we are born, the suitcase is empty.

With our birth, though, the Self (Ego), which is everything we

Learn,

And Believe to be true, after we are born, begins to fill this suitcase

up.

With each interaction we have, the suitcase becomes heavier,

As it begins to become cluttered with the baggage we accumulate,

From all the erroneous things we have Learned during our lives.

The heavier the suitcase becomes, the dimmer our Light gets

And the more we will have to unpack when we Awake

And begin our Journey toward Enlightenment.

In the suitcase are all the false self-centered truth's

Learned by the Ego (Self) and Accepted by the child as they are

growing up.

Though it does not take very long to fill the suitcase (Usually during

the first 5 years of life),

It may take the rest of their life, if at all, to Find Their Light again,

Unpack the suitcase and return to the inner peace and understanding

They once knew before the suitcase began to fill.

Let us all therefore strive to keep our children's suitcase lighter

During the early years of their life, allowing their light to remain

brighter

And their journey through life easier and more meaningful.

The Lie

As soon as we are born, the Lie begins.

Our Socialization teaches us to Accept the Mores of Society

And Our Importance in the world.

We learn those who are famous, wealthy, have important jobs,

A certain skin color, religion, sex or any other comparisons we

Learned

Defined Superiority in the world, are more Successful and Better

than others.

Nothing could be further from the truth.

In truth, our Egocentric upbring is the cause of Hatred, Greed, War,

Climate Change, Murder, Prejudice and so many other Negative

problems

Present in the world both today and throughout history.

The Truth is No One is more important than another,

Regardless of their Accomplishments in Life.

What defines the Truth is Everyone's Journey Through Life

Being as Valuable as our Own, Sharing the resources of the planet

Equally,

Allowing Every Life to Flourish, be Important, Successful and

Meaningful.

The Prism

When we are first born, before we are socialized and Taught what to

Believe,

The Light refracted through the Prism of Life is Pure White.

This White Light emerges due to the inherent

Unconditional Love present Within each life.

As we Learn how we are supposed to act and treat each other,

The white light of the Prism is dispersed into an infinite number of

colors.

The more we Accept what we Learn and are Taught

By society how we should Act and Treat others, the murkier the reflected

Colors of the rainbow, flowing through the Prism, become.

The Darker the light emerging from the Prism, the more challenging

life becomes.

Most problems, and many illnesses, experienced around the world,

Both now and throughout history, happen when a majority see

A Darkened light emerging through the Prism of Life.

As we Awaken, begin to question what we have been Taught and

Believed to be true (Ego), the colors we see reflected

Through the Prism begin to Lighten

As we start to reject much of what we once Believed.

The Lighter the colors observed on the other side of the Prism

The more Peaceful, Loving, and Meaningful our life will become.

And with this change in colors, a true understanding about

The Meaning of Life will be realized.

How Much is a Life Worth?

The going rate for a body, including the elements it is composed of

is just $1.

Is that what each life is worth?

Does having Wealth, Fame, a Prestigious Job, being a certain Race,

Religion, Sex or anything else differentiating us from each other

Make one life worth more than another?

These questions must be answered by anyone seeking to Awaken

and become Enlightened.

If your answer to these questions is Yes,

Your Spiritual Journey has not yet begun.

If, however, you begin to question how much a life is worth

Truly Believing and Accepting each life is Equally Important,

Despite Any perceived Learned differences,

Then you have Awoken and begun your Journey Towards

Enlightenment.

The End of Life

After we have lived our lives, as we approach death,

It is common to reexamine how our life went.

Did we live a "successful" life?

The end of life offers a unique opportunity to do this, because at this

time,

The Ego (Self) loosens its influence on us,

And the Spirit becomes our predominant reviewer.

At this point in the cycle of life, it no longer matters how much

Money we made, the size of the house we lived in,

The job we had, or anything else associated with success,

As dictated in the world by the Ego.

We are all finally equal now and we judge our success

Through a different prism: that of the Spirit.

When we review our lives, what we had thought was success

Often holds a different meaning now.

It is at this time, especially during the last few days of our life,

We come to the realization what we thought was important

Really was not.

All the material things we accumulated, friends we had, places we
visited,

Jobs we worked, amount of money we made, or any other
comparison

You can think of, which belongs in the world in which we had lived,

Becomes Meaningless.

It is at that moment, the moment where the Ego

Has minimal Control over our actions and decisions,

The true Meaning of Life finally becomes evident.

It is then, despite how strongly the Ego may have influenced our life
before,

The opportunity to view our life in a different way presents itself.

At this time in our life, primarily viewing our lives

Through the eyes of our Spirit, we may find we have many regrets.

We begin to understand the Selfish pleasures in the world

We had sought were not very important.

As death becomes evident, we finally realize none of that matters.

When we die, unless our culture is like that of the ancient Egyptians,

Our body will be buried or cremated and nothing we accumulated

During our lifetime will accompany us.

Our body will then be placed in a coffin or urn, just like every other

Person who dies, regardless of their stature or their lifetime

accomplishments.

At that moment, just before we die, we finally understand

We truly are all equal.

No one was ever better than another.

Race, money, prestige no longer matter.

As we get closer to our death, it becomes evident the path the Ego

had

Us follow to find success and happiness may have not been the right path after all.

The fear, hatred, and prejudice we once felt are no longer important

to us,

Not because we are going to die, but because "It Never Did Matter".

I Am Alone

Surrounded by a Sea of People I pass many others,

Barely noticing my Existence.

Within, I feel Empty, Lost, Afraid of Everything

Needing to prove my Worth every day.

I constantly Worry, wanting to be Happy, Successful,

Be able to survive in the world providing everything my family and

I

Need to be safe, enjoying the best things life has to offer.

I'm afraid to think too much.

If I do, I may realize, from the moment of our birth until we die,

We each truly are Alone in the world.

The Journey Through Life was always meant to be solitary,

Searching for answers Never able to be found in the world.

To find your Answers, to be Happy and Successful, to not be Alone,

Seek your company Within first,

Only then Sharing it without Fear with all others.

Inner Voices

We each have two voices we hear Within.

One, coming from our Mind, is loud,

Often misguided, telling us what to do and say.

The words uttered from our mind, result from what we Learned in

life,

Determining our beliefs, prejudices and how we view the world.

(Ego)

The other voice comes from our Heart.

This voice is inherent, present in every life.

Many call this voice our "Higher-Self". (Spirit)

Its messages give our life meaning.

Though both voices will remain with us throughout our life,

We may choose which voice to Hear.

Listen mostly to the quieter voice, softly whispering its message of

Love,

Rather than the louder voice from the mind, which, though

necessary,

Is the cause of many illnesses and most of the

Problems and inequalities seen throughout the world.

Look Beyond

When we look at and talk to someone what do we see and hear?

Do we see their appearance, the clothes they are wearing,

The color of their skin, or any of the many other traits

We judge another by (Ego).

Do we hear what they are saying, the words

Answering our questions or as they tell us their opinion.

Is there more than what we see and hear?

Our opinions, often formed when we are young,

Direct our interactions and how we view the world.

It is only when you look Beyond your vison and thoughts,

We see the worth of someone.

Look Within Their Soul to know another,

Revealing their Essence (Spirit) to discover who they truly are.

Who Am I?

Am I the person you see, hear, touch or I am I something else?

Am I the many roles I have been assigned by society?

A Father, Husband, Son, Daughter, Janitor, President,

Male, Female, White, Black, Asian, Gay, Straight or

Any of the many other designations we are defined as by society

As we Accept these choices we Learned to be true and have been

given.

Perhaps I am more than this.

I Am Spirit, as Every life is.

Our body is just a shell housing who we Truly Are.

We are the same, equally experiencing life.

Our appearance, job, education, race, religion, fame, wealth

Or any other apparent difference between us means little.

Who Am I?

I Am You and We Are All One.

Do Better

When we harm another with unkind words, take advantage of them

in any way,

Needing to prove we are smarter, more important than they,

We may fleetingly succeed in our effort.

In reality, though, the injury hurts both, resulting in a world of Fear,

Hate and Darkness.

We must always strive to Help, not Harm, each other.

There is Never a reason to demean another.

We each must Do Better, treat all others with Kindness, Respect and

Empathy,

Ushering in a new era of Peace, Love and Light.

Spiritual Insanity

Psychology defines insanity as a severely disordered state of the
mind.

Albert Einstein defined insanity as doing the same thing

Over and over, expecting different results.

What is the cause of Spiritual Insanity?

Spiritual Insanity is caused by living in an egocentric world,

Where war, hunger, homelessness, climate change, greed, prejudice,

Fear, hate exist, Accepting the Reality and Helplessness these
conditions cause.

We therefore settle into a pattern of self-preservation,

Concerned only for Our survival and Success in the world.

We have the ability Now to feed everyone, get rid of hunger, give
medications

To the poor for treatable illnesses, house those without shelter,

Treat climate change by accepting green alternatives,

Embrace Unconditional Love over Hate and Fear, get rid of the

causes of war

By equally sharing our resources.

What prevents us from doing this: Greed and Fear.

It is Not too late to treat the causes of Spiritual Insanity,

Though our window for change may be rapidly closing.

The time for change is Now.

Unless we Aggressively tackle the causes of Spiritual Insanity

Together

And rid society of the above scourges, there may not be

An inhabitable world left for our children to flourish in.

𝔄 𝔖mile and a 𝔎ind 𝔚ord

Each of us can affect the life of another, even briefly.

Treating others with a Smile and sincere Kindness, not influenced by

Wanting something in return, can alter the

Direction of not only one life, but the world.

This kind-hearted gesture Awakens in others,

An inherent memory present Within every life.

A memory we all once knew before we were exposed

To chaos in the world, before we were Socialized to Accept the

Many untruth's we were Taught and Believed to be True after we were born.

If enough people begin to share a Smile and Kind Word Selflessly,

Perhaps the newly Awakened person we first encountered

Will share this gesture with others, continuing ad infinitum.

To change the world, perhaps we can start simply by being Nice to each other,

By Sharing a Smile and a Kind Word.

Mid Life Crisis

After someone Awakens, there is often a difficult period of transition.

That person begins to question everything in their life.

Many people go through a Mid Life Crisis at this time.

They are confused, questioning everything they Learned and once Believed to be True.

There is a Gnawing feeling within they no longer can ignore, coming from their very core.

It is their Spirit attempting to communicate with them,

Making them question the Egoistic path in life they are on.

Finally reaching a point no longer able to ignore

This feeling, they have no choice but to make changes in their life.

"They Awake".

Friendships and relationships might fade away, their job may appear unsatisfying,

As they now may have little in common with those still Asleep.

They begin a journey to find Meaning in their Life.

A journey leading them to rediscover their Spirit within.

The Twilight of Life

As I sit on my porch on a cold winter day, in the Twilight of my

Life,

I reflect on what is important in life.

I look at the many struggles others, as well as I, had.

The wars, hunger, homelessness, greed, fear, hate, prejudice,

Life changing loss of job/divorce/illness/death or

Any number of other challenges I have seen during my life.

I now understand how unnecessary many of these difficulties were.

We do Not have to face life Alone, as we are

Taught and Learn to do when we are young.

Yet Most Do.

Instead, Sharing hardships equally, caring and

Loving others Unconditionally, understanding and Accepting

The importance of Every life, will negate many of these

Struggles and negative emotions, allowing our world to Evolve,

Ushering in, for our children, a world where

Love and Hope dominate Fear and Despair.

How to Raise a Happy Child

Bring up children to believe in the goodness of life,

To share Selflessly, Foster Respect and Love for all others,

regardless of any

Perceived Learned differences we are Taught and Accept as true.

Teach our children to find their path and Happiness in life,

Not in the world, but from their Spirit Within.

Then to share that Love Unselfishly with all others.

Every Life is Beautiful

It matters not what someone looks like, their race, color, sex,

religion,

Wealth, appearance, job or anything else we judge others by.

Every life is unique, beautiful in every way.

Our differences only help us, creating a montage,

A mosaic that together make us all stronger.

Despite any flaws we may have, embrace each other with Love

rather than

Judgment improving the future for Everyone sharing our planet.

The Journey Towards Spirituality

The journey through life, towards Spirituality,

Is very difficult, long, and often lonely.

There are a lot of frustrations you will encounter as you

Continue to live and deal with others who remain Asleep.

Every one of us Can Change the World

Around us by Sharing our Love Selflessly.

Though the Journey is challenging, we must Not give up.

For at the end of the Spiritual path lies Meaning, Inner Peace

And a true understanding about Life's Purpose.

Where are the Answers?

Do not look to others to bring

Happiness and answers about life (Ego).

They will Never be found there.

These must First be found Within (Spirit),

Then shared without cause

With all others.

The Mask

We learn, often when we are young children,

How to hide our true emotions behind a protective

Mask we all wear, becoming very adept at hiding

Almost all our feelings from Others and, often, even from

Ourselves.

Masks help us survive in the world and allow our responses

To different situations be socially acceptable.

It is not easy to continually wear a Mask.

The larger the Mask and the more of our face it covers,

The greater the problems we will have in our life and

The more Stress and Anxiety we will experience and feel.

We must all strive to rip off the Mask

Preventing us from reaching our full potential.

By doing so, allowing us to finally Embrace and

Experience Life as it was meant to be.

The Simple Message We Are Here to Learn

Fear, Hate, Prejudice. Hunger, Homelessness, Climate Change.

None of these things and so much more need exist today.

Every man-made emotion and problem results from accepting

The status quo, the belief we are each better and more deserving

than another.

"We Are Not".

In truth, we are all one, every life equally important,

Deserving to be treated with Respect and Love.

This is the simple message we are here to learn,

This is The Meaning of Life.

Living a Successful Life

Is "Success" living to old age, making a lot of money,

Having a prestigious job, a family, big house and

Being able to do the best things life has to offer?

How many people have accepted this Egocentric definition of

success?

How many wealthy people, who have everything, are miserable and

in pain?

How many of us feel the same way, as we struggle, every day,

through life?

There is another definition of success though, one much less

recognized.

Success involves Sharing the inherent unconditional Love

(Love given without expectation of receiving anything in return),

Selflessly With all Others.

Instead of wanting only Success for ourselves, we want success for

Everyone.

The former definition for success leads to many challenges in life.

The latter leads to True Happiness, Inner Peace

And to having led a Meaningful "Successful" Life.

We Are Each Other's Teachers

Every person we meet, regardless how brief, affects our life.

A small part of their Spirit, their Essence, remains with us

Changing, if only slightly, the direction our life will take.

Each one of us, therefore, can Change the World

By Sharing our Authentic Self (Spirit) with others.

We Are Each Other's Teachers.

Let us, therefore, make certain the messages we Share are Positive,

Benefiting Everyone's Journey Through Life, helping each other

Selflessly,

Leaving the world for our Children better then when we first began

our journey.

The Spirit Guide

Within every life lies a Spirit Guide.

Whether you call this guide a Spirit/ Soul/ God or anything else,

It does Not matter.

It is an Ethereal being meant to give our lives Meaning.

Awakening begins when we first begin to sense its presence

questioning

If the messages we Learned as we were growing up were True.

Enlightenment happens when we Accept Everything

We were Taught and Believed to be true was Not.

To live a Meaningful Life, Listen quietly and

Follow the path of your Spirit Guide.

The Journey

We each follow a different path on our Journey Through Life.

Though there are an endless number of turns in the road detouring

us each

In an infinite number of directions, the destination is the same.

Uniting with our Spirit Within, sharing its unconditional Love

With others will complete our journey

Bringing Meaning and Understanding to our lives.

God

The belief in God influences many people throughout the world.

Therefore, the awareness of God must not be ignored.

Whether you call God Spirit, Soul, Essence or by any other name,

This ethereal being has been the subject of much discussion

throughout time.

Though God should unite us, often it does not.

All life, regardless of religion or any existing beliefs, is Important.

No one life is more important than another.

There is a small piece of God Within every life,

Connecting each life to the other.

It is only when we Share this part of us Selflessly with each other,

Will the Spiritual Evolution of our planet finally be realized.

Each Life is Extraordinary

We are all one in a crowd of many hidden from view by the

multitude.

Yet each life is extraordinary, unique,

Having the ability to change the world,

Not by their accomplishments or prestige, but by sharing their Love

With others, changing their lives forever by doing so.

To the Children of the World

As you are growing up, you will notice life can appear to be very

challenging.

The world is not always a very nice place to live in.

You will see many things that make you wonder

Why bad things happen to so many.

You will see people who do not have enough food to eat or a place

to live,

And others, who do not like someone because they are different.

Regardless of what color your skin is, the country you live in,

Your beliefs, religion, or any other differences there are,

It is important you do Not believe anyone is better

Or more important than anyone else.

Every Life is Equally Important, regardless of any

Perceived differences there are between us.

Living a good life has Nothing to do with the job you have,

The amount of money you make, if you are famous or

Anything else you may hear about when you are growing up.

Rather, the only important thing is that you are a Good person.

Be someone who cares about others feelings, helping them

whenever you can,

Treating everyone with kindness and love, even if they do Not treat

you that way.

You will find there are many in the world who are unhappy,

Afraid and worry only about themselves.

Please, do Not be like them.

You can change the world if you simply Listen to the quiet voice

In your heart and share that message with everyone.

Embrace life with awe. Be kind to everyone.

Share the goodness in your heart with those who are different or

struggling.

And, most importantly, treat others like you want to be treated.

If you do this, you will be happy.

Choose Not to live in a world where everyone is afraid,

Worrying only about themselves.

Instead, be generous, empathetic, loving,

Respectful, humble, patient, honest, compassionate, kind,

Positive, grateful, hopeful, and optimistic about life.

Be courageous. care about others feelings,

Be friendly and help them if they are different or in need.

If you do this, you may find your life will be happy and meaningful.

The path you choose through life will decide the future of the world.

The older generations have Not done a very good job

Taking care of our planet and each other.

It is up to you, therefore, to make the changes

That must be made, by choosing the right path in life.

We Are All Equal, Important and Connected

It does not matter what Job you have, how much Money you make,

The Color of your Skin, Where you Live, your Race, Religious

preference,

Sex, Sexual preference, or any other comparison we may make.

We are All Equal, Important and Connected.

Only when Everyone succeeds in life, regardless of their looks,

beliefs

Or any other differences, will Life truly have Meaning.

What Happened to the Hippie Generation?

(Though this is written about the Hippie generation,

it could just as easily be written about Any generation)

When we were young, we were Idealistic and going to Change the

World.

We understood the Meaning of Life was to

Share our Love Selflessly with All others.

Sex, Drugs and Rock & Roll was our mantra. Life was Good.

As we got older though, our lives became more challenging.

We had families, bills and began to Forget why we were born.

Many of us began to Accept societies definition of Success.

Rather than Selflessly focusing on what was Best for Everyone,

We began to concentrate only on our accomplishments and

What was best for our family and ourselves.

Instead of sharing our Love freely, without conditions, with all others,

As we once inherently knew when we were young,

Our job, amount of money we made, material possessions and

Other worldly things soon defined our existence.

As our generation begins to enter the twilight of our lives

It is Not time to just Reminisce about our youth.

Instead, it is time to Finish what we started by spreading

Unconditional Love, Peace and Light around the world.

We Must leave our Children a world they can flourish in.

A world where they can share these idealistic Spiritual values not only

With their children, but with each other and all life on our planet as well.

We Must Not Live in the Past Any Longer.

It is time for All of us to rise, change the

Direction of our world, as we once hoped to do.

If we do not, our lives will have been lived in Vain leaving our

children

And grandchildren an uninhabitable world of Fear, Hate and

Distrust.

How Do You Know When You Are Awake?

Instead of seeing only the worse in people,

You will now begin to see the good in others.

Instead of Darkness, you will see Light,

Instead of Helplessness, you will want to Help others,

Instead of Accepting living in a world of Fear,

You will want to help change the world,

Allowing all others to live in a world of

Love, Compassion and Hope instead.

What is Enlightenment?

Once you Accept the Spirit, rather than the Ego

As your primary guide through life, Fear in your life vanishes,

No longer dictating your life choices.

Spirit's path is Love, unconditionally shared with all.

With this Acceptance comes Enlightenment.

The Dream

When we are born, the dream begins.

For most, it will continue unabated until the moment of their death.

Everything we See, Learn about, and Accept as real

Becomes a repetitive dream we have every day.

We remain asleep when we Accept what we Learned was true,

Believing there is nothing we can do to change what is happening

Around the world, including the many hardships experienced by so

many.

There are those who begin to Awaken from their sleep,

Start to question if what they have been dreaming about and

Believed to be true throughout their lives was real.

"It Was Not".

We finally wake up completely when we truly understand

Nothing we had dreamed about was genuine (Enlightenment).

It was all a myth, created by our Ego, to control our lives,

Convincing us of Our importance.

To Awaken from your deep slumber, to begin to open your eyes,

Lifting you out of your unrelenting dream, listen to the

Quiet voice within, follow its direction, changing the

False path through life your dream had you Believe was real.

"It Never Was".

When You See Another

When you see another do you only look at their appearance?

When you talk with another do you only hear their words?

To genuinely know another look deeper,

Beyond the superficial layers we each project,

By seeing and hearing their Essence within, embracing who

They truly are rather than the illusion they project to the world.

Humility

No one, regardless of wealth, prestige or any other perceived

Difference is better or more important than another.

Every life is equally important deserving

To be treated with Respect and Kindness.

Though many have Learned they are better than another,

Due to the color of their skin, sex, religion, or any of the many other

Distinctions between us, They Never Have Been.

Believing and Accepting we are superior to others leads to all

The wars, prejudice and hatred existing throughout time.

To change the future, leaving a better world for our children,

Recognize every life's value, treating each as we hope to be treated

ourselves.

Do Not Fear Death

It is not important when you die; it is how you live that will define

your life.

Wealth, Material possessions, living to old age, or anything else we

Learn and

Believe is important to have led a good life, will not impede death.

As death approaches and you review your life, often, many realize

None of the things we thought would define our life mattered,

That our life was not meaningful or important.

A poor homeless child, dying at a very young age, Accepting the

Messages

From their Spirit within before their early demise, may have led a more

Profound life then one much older and "successful" than they were.

It is how we live our life, sharing the message of eternal Love

Within

That will define our life when death inevitably approaches.

Wɧat Do You See?

When you look at the world, what do you see?

Do you see Light or Darkness? Love or Hate?

Happiness or Sadness? Hope or Fear?

Allowing life (Ego) to dictate your future, accepting all the false

things

We learned were true, you will only see Darkness, Hate, Sadness

and Fear.

Allowing your Spirit, however, your Inner Voice, to direct your path

through life,

Light, Love, Happiness and Hope will be seen

In every person and every challenge you meet in life.

The Battle Within

Within every life a gnawing deep need exists

To discover a reason, a meaning for our existence.

There must be more to life than just making money, having a family,

Enjoying ourselves, buying nice clothes and other material

possessions.

Though we may have all these things, it does

Not satisfy an unsatiable need we feel within.

We go through life often asleep, unaware there is more than

Doing all the things we Learned will allow us to have a successful

life.

Those asleep, often manifest physical symptoms, such as depression,

anxiety

And, around mid-age, may go through a mid-life crisis, as they

reevaluate their life,

Knowing there is something wrong but not understanding what it is.

The physical symptoms result from the internal battle between the

Ego,

What we learned in life, and the Spirit within, our Higher-Self.

Though both are important to thrive, it is only when you embrace

Your Spirit as your primary guide through life

You Awake and your life finally begins to make sense.

How Many Must Die?

How many more children must die before we wake up from our

slumber?

How many men, women, families must be destroyed?

The world, all life, is on a precipice.

If we continue on the destructive path we are on,

Climate change, Nuclear war, or some other man-made catastrophe

Will end the suffering of all life, leaving only an uninhabitable

Empty shell where a once vibrant planet had existed.

To step back from the abyss, we must stop the needless deaths of so

many,

Reject Hate and Fear, replacing it instead with Love and Hope.

We Are Each Part of a Whole

We are one of many, we each are part of a whole.

Every life is unique, special, yet we share a common purpose.

Though we may appear different, have distinct personalities and

beliefs,

We are linked by a universal entity present within every life.

Look past what you see, judge, hear, believe (Ego) to the Spirit/Soul

within another.

It is there you will finally understand we are all related, we are one,

Part of a collective, alive to Help each other spreading

Love and Hope as we journey through life together.

Look Deeper

When you talk, see, hear another look beyond

The petty superficial facade they present.

Talk to their true self, Within every life.

See the beauty they radiate from within.

Hear the words of Love emanating from their heart.

Everything else is an illusion, a lie, a myth Learned

After we were born, Accepted as real, dictated by others as truth.

"It Never Was".

To truly know another, Look Deeper.

What Defines Us?

Are we what we are Taught?

Are we our sex, race, religion, job, or anything else we learned we

are? (Ego)

Does that define us?

Or are we more, something else?

Are we our Spirit, Soul, a Piece of God, present within every life,

There to help give meaning and guide us on our journey through

life? (Spirit)

"We Are Both".

We must decide which, our Ego or Spirit, to primarily follow

through life.

Simply look at the world, both today and throughout history,

To see the results of allowing our Ego to dominate our life.

If, however, we choose to follow the direction of our Spirit,

The possibilities are endless. There is no more time to wait.

A choice must be made now: Extinction (Ego) or Evolution (Spirit).

Which we choose to predominately follow will

Determine the future of all life on our planet.

The Fork in the Road

There are but two paths we may choose through life.

Though we each must travel our own individual journey,

We have a choice which path we may take.

The path of Fear (Ego), which represents accepting

Everything we Learned in life as true,

Or the path of Love (Spirit), present within every life,

Representing the unlimited possibilities living in a

Loving, selfless world permits.

One path leads to struggle, stress, unhappiness, confusion.

The other to understanding, contentment and peace.

To find the path you desire when you come to the fork in the road

Choose the steeper more difficult path, accepting the messages

You Hear Within rather than the ones you were taught

To Believe were true when you were a child.

Why?

Why do so many struggle? Why is life so difficult?

Why are people hungry, homeless, harm others?

Why do I feel so unhappy, stressed, anxious? Why am I alive?

Life is a gift, a spiritual journey meant to be shared,

Helping each other when we face challenges.

It doesn't make sense.

We choose which path through life to pursue.

Why do we choose to live in Fear (Ego)

Rather than with Love (Spirit)?

Why?

Rain

We are like the drops of rain, gently falling from the overcast sky.

Each drop is slight, though together we provide sustenance for all

life.

Despite any achievements we may have if we attain them alone

Concerned only for ourselves, just as a single raindrop is

insignificant,

Though we may be successful, we will continue to live

In a world of Fear (Ego).

If, however, our achievements are shared equally with others,

As with the many raindrops that combine together to sustain life,

We will live in a world of Love (Spirit) instead.

The Gift

There is a gift waiting to be claimed by each of us.

It has always been there, hidden from sight

By the many distractions we encounter after we are born (Ego).

This gift lies Within everything alive,

Patiently hoping to be Rediscovered (Spirit).

Once it is unwrapped, it imbues the whole being

In a bright unencumbered light, radiating an aura of

Serenity, Love and Understanding.

After this gift is opened, its contents Must be shared

For all to enjoy and benefit from.

Doing so, will fulfill our life journey's purpose,

Ushering in a new era of Hope and Peace.

The Truth About Life

It does not matter how wealthy we are, the amount of

Material possessions, job, prestige, or anything else we Learned,

To determine if we have lived a successful life (Ego).

Having these things may present an illusion our life is meaningful

and worthwhile.

In reality, though, they are simply superficial, artificial relics of a

Deceptive reality we are Taught, Accept and Believe is true when

we are young.

Look deeply into the Heart (Spirit) of a sentient life.

Within the beating heart, rests the truth about life.

This is where all the answers lie and the Meaning of Life will be

discovered.

Is There is More to Life?

As we each journey through life, are we content with who we are?

If we have a good life, family, material possessions, should we

accept

Our life is successful, reaching the goals we Learned, Accepted

When we were young and Taught us how our life should be led?

Could there be More to Life?

Sit silently, look into your eyes in a mirror or reflecting pond.

If you do, you may see a sentient being Within returning your gaze,

Attempting to tell you there is More to Life.

You may see there is an entire part of life

You have ignored and not explored.

A part that will help you discover Love, Inner Peace, Hope

And allow you to truly discover the Meaning of Life.

Ubuntu - The Divine Spark of Kindness

"I Am Because We Are".

Ubuntu is an African philosophy meaning Love, Truth, Peace,

Happiness, Eternal Optimism, Inner Goodness and

All other positive inherent traits present Within each life.

Gentleness, Hospitality, Empathy, Compassion, Friendliness,

Generosity

Are just some of these divine Spiritual qualities shared with others.

Ubuntu is the Essence, the divine spark of Kindness, present Within

every life,

Shared without motive, for the benefit of all.

Always strive to live in a world where Ubuntu is the norm,

Allowing our children to grow up and live in a world of Peace,

Love, and Light, rather than the only world they have ever known,

A world of War, Hate and Fear.

Are We Better?

Is one person better than another?

Is one species, though dominant, better than a different kind of life?

Is one life, regardless of its importance, worth more than another's?

We are taught our species is superior, one life more valuable,

And we, individually, are greater than other life forms and each

other.

We Awaken when we question if this is true.

We become Enlightened when we understand

"It Never Was".

My Barrier

It is difficult to let down my barrier preventing anyone,

Including those closest to me, pierce my impenetrable shell.

This barrier protects me from the pain perpetuated by others,

Needing to prove their superiority by their words and actions.

It also isolates me though, from discovering and revealing

Who I truly am, my true self.

I therefore go through life alone, unable to share my

Love Within, leaving me living an artificial, superficial life,

One devoid of understanding or meaning.

It is quite difficult, though possible to lower our barrier,

Allowing us to find Meaning and true Love during our life.

To do so, close your eyes, listen, Awaken

And follow the new path through life you will discover.

How Do You See the World?

When you look at the world do you see darkness or light?

Are there endless struggles as we strive alone to survive

Or is there a shared journey, together helping each other

Through life's many challenges?

Is there fear or courage, hate or love, prejudice or acceptance?

Though it may not appear we control our destiny,

How we view others and the world is a choice.

Choose to see life's beauty rather than malice,

Awakening you on a journey of self-discovery.

What Happens When You Awaken?

Most go through life Asleep,

Doing everything they Learned (Ego) they were supposed to do.

They went to school, got a job, started a family, bought a house, traveled,

Made a lot of money, bought many nice material things to make their life easier.

You Awaken when you begin to question if what you had Learned was true.

If there may be another more important reason you were born,

A reason you cannot fully understand, though know is significant.

As you begin to reexamine your life, your many successes you had,

You begin to feel your life, regardless of your achievements, lacks meaning.

When this happens, your life will change forever

As you embark on a new journey, a Journey of Awakening (Spirit).

The World We Are Leaving Our Children

War, Hunger, Poverty, Climate Change. Hate, Fear, Prejudice,

Greed.

Too many problems to list.

Not one of these man-made challenges and emotions need exist.

By sharing the bounties of the earth, respecting all life and our

planet equally,

Living our lives with Love rather than Fear

We could leave our children a world they would thrive in,

A world of Hope, Peace, and Love rather than a world of Despair,

War and Hate.

We can change the world Now. All we lack is the will to do.

To give our children a chance to find true Happiness and

Meaning in their lives, to lessen the burdens they may face in their

lives,

We must embrace a new paradigm of life, one where every life is

equally valued,

Treated with respect and empathy rather than malice and

indifference.

It is our choice which world we will leave our children.

I pray we choose wisely.

Following the Wrong Path in Life

The emotional pain many feel is the cause of anxiety, stress,

depression

And many other challenges we each face in life as we strive

To survive and find joy and happiness in our lives.

This pain is caused by our Learned reactions to different events and

situations

We are or have been exposed to during our life (Ego).

We do Not have to confront every trauma or

Negative event in our life to diminish this pain.

We only need recognize the pain is caused by following the wrong

path through life;

The path we were taught to Believe and Accepted as real as we were

growing up.

To change our path, to rid ourselves of the pain, to find true

happiness and

Meaning in our lives, quiet your mind, Listen and follow the advice

you Hear (Spirit).

A Part of Us

Within every life there is a Spirit/Soul/Essence/God.

It does not matter what you call it. It Connects all of us to each

other.

This part of us represents our Higher-Self, the genuine Love,

Within each life, meant to be shared with all others.

With every interaction, regardless how brief, we share a small part

Of our Spirit with another, changing both your and their life forever.

Even if we physically die, this encounter, despite how fleeting, will

live

Within them in perpetuity, enriching each in their journey through

life.

Accepting this, sharing this part of us selflessly with others is

Enlightenment,

The reason we are born, the lesson we are here to learn,

The Meaning of Life.

Look for the Good

Do you see the good in others or do you seek out their faults?

Do you have a need to prove you are better than another or

Can you accept the unique majesty of others?

Though there are many man made problems existing throughout the

world,

We each have a choice how we see and treat others.

Do not judge another, rather accept every life,

Embracing the uniqueness and Love within each.

Look for the good, discard the rest.

Help all those in need with kindness and empathy.

By doing so, we can not only change ourselves,

But we can change the future of the world itself.

Our Lens

Viewing life through a tinted lens, reveals an irredeemable

World of Fear, Hate, Greed, and Prejudice,

War, Hunger, Homelessness, and Climate Change.

A world whose negative emotions and problems are too vast to list.

For some, their lens is so dark, they are blind.

Others, though their lens does not totally blind them,

Still have difficulty seeing the world clearly.

Our blackened lens, begins to lighten when we start to view

The world with Love, rather than Fear (Awaken).

Sharing this Love selflessly further lightens the lens we see

The world through, until our lens becomes clear.

And with this clarity comes Enlightenment.

𝕿𝖍𝖊 𝕾𝖕𝖎𝖗𝖎𝖙

The Spirit, residing Within every life, gives our lives Meaning.

It teaches us respect, compassion, empathy, love, caring,

Selflessness, understanding, and all other innate positive values.

Its message is: We are all in life's journey together.

Only when we All Succeed, Helping each other unselfishly,

Will our lives have Meaning and Value.

Choices in Life

Choose Not to live in a world of Fear, worrying only about

ourselves.

This is the cause of hate, war, prejudice, hunger, climate change,

homelessness,

Anxiety, stress and all other man-made preventable challenges.

Choose instead to live in a world of Love, worrying equally about

every life,

Ensuring everyone's success and happiness.

Choosing Love Over Fear will eliminate all the needless egocentric

hardships,

By introducing a new era of Peace and Cooperation.

The Ego and the Spirit

Are they opposites, the Ying & Yang Within every life?

As one Awakens, the Ego begins to loosen its hold

On our journey through life and the Spirit begins to assert its

presence.

This continues as we travel further on the path towards

Enlightenment.

As the Spirit becomes stronger, the Ego lessens its influence

Until we reach a point where the Spirit becomes more dominant

In our decisions, actions and path than the Ego.

It is at that point, Enlightenment truly begins.

Our Prayer

When You Open Your Eyes, what Do You See?

Do you see a world influenced by the Self (Ego),

By what we Learned and Accepted as true?

A world of Fear, Hate, Prejudice, Distrust.

A world of War, Hunger, Homelessness, Climate Change.

Or do you see a world influenced by the Spirit Within.

A world of Unconditional Love, Hope, Equality, Empathy.

A world of Peace, where hunger, homelessness, and climate change

No longer exist due to the Shared concern for every life.

When You Open Your Eyes, which world will you see?

Our prayer is when we Open our Eyes we choose what

We see wisely for the future of our children and all life on our

planet.

The Legacy of Greed

To solve poverty, as well as hunger, homelessness and

Numerous other problems observed throughout the world,

There needs to be a fundamental Shift in Consciousness.

We live in a world of Greed.

The only way to Solve poverty, as well as all other problems

Secondary to Greed, is by sharing all the resources on the planet

Equally.

Every life is essential. No One is more important than another.

To rid the world of Greed, we must Selflessly Accept this paradigm,

Embracing the belief what is best for Everyone

Is more important than what is best for just Ourselves.

You are Never Truly Alone

We are each Accompanied through life by a Spirit Guide.

The answers we seek enabling us to embrace Inner Peace,

Love and Meaning in our Life, may Never be found in the World

By looking outside or by being with another person.

The answers may only be found looking Within,

Where the Spirit Guide exists.

Listen quietly to the Voice you Hear,

Then Share its message with all others.

Love

Everyone wants love.

Regardless of who you are, this one emotion

Has been desired throughout recorded history.

Yet it is your definition of Love that will decide if you will truly

find it.

There are two ways to view love.

One, is what we Learned love was as we were growing up,

By watching TV, reading books, and observing those around us.

Learned Love is conditional.

It is given with the expectation we will get something back in return;

Often this is the return of love back.

The other way to view love is Inherent Love.

This love comes from Within and is given freely and selflessly

Without expectation of receiving anything in return.

This pure form of love comes from our Spirit/Soul

And is what Love is meant to be and feel like.

To be able to discover Inherent Love, you need to be truly
concerned

About Everyone's success in life, rather than only your success.

Simply looking at the world today and throughout history,

It is obvious what form of love is and has always been dominant.

It is up to each of us to spread Love Selflessly, to care equally for
everyone's

Success in life, for the Spiritual Evolution of our species to occur.

If we do not, the world we are leaving our children is destined for
failure.

Clouds

I gaze at the clouds in the sky.

They are white, grey and some appear much darker.

Just as clouds, we each go through periods in our life

Reflecting our understanding of our purpose in life.

Our clouds are darkest when we are stressed,

Trying to survive the many challenges life presents us (Ego).

They lighten slightly, becoming grey, when we begin to wonder

If perhaps there is a deeper meaning to life (Awaken).

As we travel further on the path, embracing the messages

We Hear Within (Spirit), the clouds begin to turn white.

On the day we finally understand and Accept the guidance that has

always

Been present Within every life, the clouds disappear,

Leaving a clear blue sky in its stead (Enlightenment).

In the Blink of an Eye

Life is quite unpredictable.

One moment, everything is going well, you are Successful,

Reaping the rewards earned by doing Everything Right.

This may all change, though, in the Blink of an Eye.

A sudden death, accident, loss of a job, divorce, war, famine,

disease,

Effects of climate change, or any number of other

Life-changing events may change the rest of your life forever.

We live in a world where this loss may be catastrophic.

To survive, we each must struggle, often mostly

Alone, to find our bearings once more.

Life does Not have to be like this.

We have only chosen to Accept the Values, Beliefs and Results

We Learned living in an Egocentric world.

There is another solution though, if anything happens to disrupt your

or

Someone's else's life, even a stranger you may not know, someone

Who may look different or have disparate beliefs than you have.

We can Help them, in their time of need, without expectation of

receiving

Any reward, simply because they are fellow travelers,

On a similar Journey Through Life as ours.

The only thing stopping us from living in such an Altruistic World

Is our Belief and Acceptance we are better, more deserving than

everyone else.

"We Are Not".

Every life is Equally Important.

To truly Change the World, we each must rise up, rejecting our

Learned beliefs,

Embracing instead the Selfless Spiritual Beliefs Within each of us,

Within every life.

Together, as one, we may succeed.

Apart, only failure and

Continuation of the unforgiving status quo will continue.

Reflections of My Life

My body has become frail. I am unable to do the things I used to do.

I now spend most of my time remembering my life, reflecting about

life in general.

When I look at the world, I wonder why?

Why is there war, indiscriminate killing, starvation, hunger,

Homelessness, prejudice, hate, fear, climate change, inequality,

And daily struggles for so many seeming to never end?

Why are some people who are Successful in life,

Have a prestigious job, wealth, and many material possessions,

Unable to find inner peace, happiness, or meaning in their lives?

And others, who appear to have very little, are happy,

And able to experience true joy?

Sitting on my porch, after much contemplation, I believe I finally

can answer this question.

Those who look to the world and others for their Happiness,

Meaning, and Success,

Who are primarily concerned for only their well-being,

Struggle Within to find these things.

Those, however, who are brought up with Love,

Having respect and equal concern for every life,

Will help end many of the man-made problems above, allowing not

Only their but all other lives to flourish and have Meaning as well.

Colors

When you look at the world are the colors you see crisp and clear,

Unimpeded by the many different hues

Altering the pure natural colors seen on a perfect day?

Most view the world, seeing a variety of hues.

Some days everything appears hazy,

Blurred by stress, anxiety, depression, and confusion.

Other days, we see a world vibrant and transparent.

To see clarity, to see the pure unobstructed colors of the world,

To truly appreciate life, share your Love and Kindness,

Genuinely caring about all others.

𝕴 𝕳𝖆𝖛𝖊 𝖆 𝕯𝖗𝖊𝖆𝖒

I Have a Dream of a World where Love, Freely Shared with others,

Is the main emotion we feel, and Consideration for the

Importance of every life is equally considered.

It is a world where there is no hunger, homelessness, or climate

change.

No fear, hatred, or prejudice.

A world where none of the many problems or negative emotions

Defining our existence throughout time are present.

It is a world where we share our resources and

Love selflessly eliminating these scourges from our planet.

Our world is at a Precipice.

To achieve such a dream, make it a reality, we all must decide to

Embrace Love over Fear, Hope over Despair and

Selflessness (Spirit) over Selfishness (Ego).

We can each decide Today to make this change.

By doing so, we can change the direction of our world forever.

You may Not believe such a dream can come true,

But I assure you it can.

We can accomplish this Now.

All we lack is the Will, Belief and Desire to do so.

When We Die

Does anyone really know, with certainty, what happens When We

Die?

There are many theories, often based on Learned religious beliefs,

Yet we will not truly find out until our death.

Much of our lives center around our uncertainty of what will happen

that day.

We therefore live our lives in "Fear", hoping to be able to live a

good life,

Focusing on Our Success in the World, material possessions, wealth,

And other things, allowing us to experience the best in life before

we die.

Looking at our declining world, now and throughout time,

With problems too numerous to mention,

We have always and continue to live life being Fearful.

Is this the world we wish for?

Perhaps it is time to change our idea of Success,

By living our lives caring and helping others, with compassion,

empathy, and concern for everyone.

If we do this, when We Die, perhaps we will find our lives have

Truly been Meaningful and Worthwhile.

Our Real Emotions

The Ego or Self may give us the Illusion of

Love and Happiness, though these feelings are false.

All Learned emotions are a Mirage.

Though they may seem real, "They Are Not".

The emotions associated with a truly Happy Meaningful Life

Come from the Spirit (our Higher Self).

Open your Heart, freely Share your Love and Happiness

Within with all others unselfishly to truly experience

What these and all other positive emotions are genuinely meant to

feel like.

Fear vs Love (Ego vs Spirit)

As we were growing up, we were Taught how to act,

What to Believe and how to Survive in the world.

If we accepted what we had Learned, as the great majority of the

world has,

We were Taught to be primarily concerned about

Ourselves, Our happiness and Our survival in the world.

We were told if we made a lot of money, we will be successful and

happy.

By accepting this Learned view of the world, we also learned to live

our lives in Fear.

And with Fear, comes many other negative emotions seen

throughout our very polarized world.

Imagine, instead, growing up where there was concern

For Everyone, rather than for only Ourselves.

Success and happiness would only happen if Everyone succeeded in

life.

By accepting this Inherent view of the world, we would live our

lives with Love.

The love I am talking about is not what we learn or read about,

Conditional love, which is given with the expectation we will

receive love back.

Rather, this Unconditional love comes from Within and is given

without reservation.

For our children and the world to flourish, we must reverse

The paradigm of life and choose to embrace Love over Fear

(Spirit over Ego).

The Facade

The Facade disguises the Real person, hidden in plain sight,

Hiding behind a Mask the Ego Taught us wear,

To Protect us when we were children, not only from everyone else,

But from ourselves as well.

We only begin to Experience life after the Mask,

The outer shell of pretense, is stripped away,

Leaving our Authentic Self (Spirit) to share our Love with all others.

Do No Harm

With Every decision we make during our life,

Our Primary guiding principle should be Do No Harm.

Whether that harm is physical, emotional, verbal, financial

Or in any other manner, it does Not matter.

Every person, every form of life, deserves to be treated

With Respect and Empathy, always considering what your

Behaviors, words and actions might bring.

Be Thoughtful before you Act or Speak.

Our actions may Help others, though they may also cause great Pain.

Let us all help bring change to the world by adopting this

One simple principle, teaching it to our children, and doing so,

Help make the world a more loving, caring home for them to live

in.

Every Life is Valuable

Inequality is frequently determined by where you are born,

If your family is rich or poor, the color of your skin, male or female,

Your sexual preference, religious beliefs, job, appearance,

education,

Or any of the many other comparisons differentiating us from each

other.

Often, wanting to Feel Superior and more Successful than others

We treat and talk to others with Disrespect due to their differences,

Making us Feel we are Better than they are.

This is the cause of all man-made problems experienced throughout

time.

If you believe this Illusion, continue following the same path

Pursued throughout millennia, nothing will change.

Wars, Hunger, Homelessness, Climate Change, Fear, Hate,

Prejudice and all the

Many other challenges experienced by so many will continue

unabated.

A radical change in Thinking and Actions is needed to alter this

dynamic.

This transformation can only happen when there is

A Darwinian Spiritual Evolution of our planet.

One where we acknowledge we Never have been better or

Superior to another, helping All Others, treating each other

With respect, Accepting every life is Important, Equal and

Connected.

Do Not Wait

When we die, the many challenges life had presented us end

As our physical body and Ego cease to exist.

Everything we accumulated during our lifetime will not

Accompany us, as we are laid to rest.

It no longer will matter if we lived a "successful" life,

Were wealthy, famous, had a prestigious job,

The color of our skin, male or female, gay or straight

Or any other comparison that can be made.

When we die, all that is left is an empty shell once housing our

Spirit/Soul.

Spirit is eternal, accompanying each of us, on our Journey Through

Life.

We Awaken when we begin to question if everything we Learned

While we were alive (Ego) is true.

We become Enlightened when we Accept None of it was.

Selflessly Embracing the Spirit's message while we are alive

Is the reason we are born, the Meaning of Life.

Do not wait until you approach death to finally understand

The lesson we are here to Learn and the Spiritual path we are meant

to follow.

Let us use our time alive Wisely, Accepting and

Unconditionally Sharing the positive Loving values of the Spirit.

With this Embrace, will come Inner Peace, knowing your life has

been Meaningful,

Making your Journey Through Life truly Successful and

Worthwhile.

A Successful Life

Success is Not prestige, wealth, or anything else

Associated with the Ego or the outside world.

Success may only be found by freeing your Spirit Within,

Then sharing its Unconditional Love,

Your Light, with all others.

I Am in Pain

There is no need to list all the challenges and Man-Made tragedies

Existing in the world today and throughout our reign on Earth.

I Am in Pain,

Knowing the numerous struggles so many have, as they strive to

Survive every day, in a deteriorating world on the verge of

Extinction.

I Am in Pain

Looking at the anguished faces of Mothers, Children and Others

Struggling in an Illusionary world whose priorities favor the

Strong, Mean and Self-Centered, rather than the Needs of Everyone.

The need to prove our superiority, not only to other species,

But to Each Other as well, proving we are better then another,

Is the cause of my Pain.

When we Awaken, we begin to question if the egocentric path

We have been following in life is right.

We become Enlightened when we Accept it is Not, realizing it is

The cause of the Pain so many experience throughout the world.

We can change this dynamic only by totally rejecting the path our

species has

Pursued from its inception, Accepting and Sharing instead the

Peaceful Selfless Loving Path of the Spirit Within.

Our Path Through Life

We each follow a different path through life;

Some paths are more challenging than others.

Our many encounters in life help form the person we become

And how we react to different situations and people,

As we interact with others we meet every day throughout our lives.

Due to our distinctive backgrounds, we each make different choices

When we are confronted with the many unique situations we

encounter every day.

For some, our responses are socially acceptable. For others they are

Not.

Regardless, we each Do the Best We Can.

We do Not have the right to judge another.

We do Not know the many challenges they have faced in their lives.

All we may do is Be there for them, Sharing our Love

To try to ease their burden and Journey Through Life.

By doing so, helping them see the world through

A prism of Light rather than Darkness,

Changing the course of their Life and the World.

Imagine

Think how our words and actions may affect

The lives of every person we interact with.

A single incident happening during a life may have a

Profound effect on someone for the rest of their life.

Imagine what life could be like if we treated each other, all Life

Forms, and

The Earth with the respect and caring we all desire for Ourselves.

Instead of Competition, there would be Cooperation.

Instead of living our lives in Fear, worrying only about Ourselves,

We would live our lives with Love and Compassion,

Worrying about Each Other.

Imagine.

Is There a Reason We Are Alive?

After we are born, we all ask that question sometime during our

Lives.

Are we Alive just to Survive, idly passing time until we get old and

die?

If we make a lot of money, own many nice possessions,

Have a family, or anything else many would say is our reason for

life,

When we prepare to die, would we feel our life was important and

worthwhile?

Or is there more to our Journey Through Life?

Most are Asleep, going through the motions, passing time,

Doing the many mundane things life offers until they die.

There are others, though, questioning if there is Meaning to Life,

Beginning to sense, Within, an unrelenting message,

Waking them from their deep slumber.

They begin to Awaken to the possibility we are born for a Reason:

To Learn, Share, Help Others Selflessly;

Reevaluating Everything we once believed to be true,

Beginning our Journey Towards Enlightenment.

The choice which path in life we each take is Ours.

To Sleep through life or begin to Wake up.

By Listening quietly to the messages Within,

The reason we are alive will become obvious.

A World of Peace

When I close my eyes, I dream of a world of Peace, Love, and

Hope.

There is no war, hate, prejudice, greed.

Everything is shared equally for the benefit of all.

Though this is not reality, It Can Be.

We have the ability Now to feed the world, clothe and house the

homeless,

Eliminate climate change, tackle all other man-made problems.

To do so, when we open our eyes, instead of seeing a world where

Only Fear dictates our actions, we see a world of Love, shared with

others

Desiring what is best for everyone, rather than only for Ourselves.

Raising Our Children with Love

What is Learned during the first five years of a child's life,

May affect their Entire Life.

The many struggles we have throughout our lives often result from

the beliefs

We Developed and Accepted during these early, impressionable

years,

When we Learn about our relationship with the world.

We then often spend the Rest of our Life undoing

The harm done during these vulnerable years.

Let us therefore strive to raise our children embracing Love instead

of Fear,

Allowing their Journey Through Life to be Meaningful and Happy.

We Must Share the Meaning of Life

When you Accept the guidance of your Spirit Within

Everything in your life changes forever.

Though the Ego, which is everything you have Learned and

Believed to be true

Since your birth, will continue to be present, to help

You navigate the everyday trials of life, it no longer dictates your

actions.

With the Spirit now as your primary guide through life, you are

Awakened.

With the Acceptance of its message you become Enlightened.

Those who truly understand this must share its message

Helping others seeking meaning in their life find it as well.

The Sky

When you look at the sky what do you see?

Do you see a crystal blue sky, without clouds disguising

The bright sun's rays when we are awake?

Do you see an infinite number of stars illuminating the night sky

Unencumbered by the bright lights below?

Or do you see dark clouds in the sky, completely covering the sun's

rays

And the stars splendor, causing havoc and suffering to our planet

below?

It is our Choice how we view the sky. It has little to do with the

weather.

Choose to see the Sky With Light rather than Darkness,

Then Share your beauty and Light with all others.

Our Baggage in Life

Each one of us has Baggage we carry from our Experiences in Life.

Our Baggage often causes us to see the World differently.

If your Baggage causes you to view the World with Fear,

Concerned only for yourself and family, your narrowed Vision of

Life

Will cloud many of your decisions and lead to an unfulfilled life.

If, however, "Despite" the Baggage you have carried in your life,

You embrace and live your life with Love, Shared Freely and

Unconditionally

With all others, your expanded Vision of Life will allow you to

Awaken,

Bringing Happiness, Inner Peace and a True Understanding of the

Meaning of Life.

Are You Your Brother's Keeper?

Is Your Life More Important Than Another's?

Should you not care about helping everyone, allowing their

Life to be easier and more Meaningful?

If you live your life in Fear, concerned only for your

Survival and Happiness your answer to the above questions is Yes.

And though you may Survive, be Successful and

Live to an Old Age, your Life will lack Meaning.

If, however, the answer to the above questions is No,

Then, though you may not be as Successful and live as long as

others

Who live their Life in Fear, your life will be Important, Meaningful

and

You will have Discovered the Lesson we are here to Learn.

We Have Always Had the Answers

The Meaning of Life cannot be found in the world

Or through being with others.

It may only be found Within, where the Spirit is,

Accompanying each of us in our Journey Through Life,

Then Sharing its Love Selflessly with all others.

Shine Your Light Brightly

Choose to Live in a world where your Light shines brightly,

Sharing with others the incredible Inner Peace and Love

Emanating from your very core Within.

Assure every life has an equal chance to

Experience and find their Light as well,

Bringing Peace, Light, and Love to the world.

Look into the Soul of Another

When you look at another, what do you see?

Is it the protective shield we place around ourself,

Hiding our true feelings from others?

When you talk to another, do you truly Hear

What they are saying or do you hear their superficial words

Disguising their thoughts within?

Look past the obvious, the façade, when you see or hear others,

Into their very Soul within, to truly get to know another by

Sharing an intimate moment together that may change

The direction of both your lives forever.

We are All Human Beings

Regardless of any comparison you can think of

Dividing us from One Another, we are all Human Beings,

Deserving to be Treated Equally, with Compassion.

Though some may believe they are Better than others

This Fallacy is a Lie, perpetrated by the Mind (Ego)

And is the cause of many Hardships experienced throughout time.

We are all Human Beings Equal in Every way,

Regardless of any Man-Made Comparison.

We are United by a common Spirit, present Within each of us.

Only by Embracing and Sharing our Spirit, helping Each

Other Selflessly will the true Meaning of Life be understood.

Always Be Kind

There is Never a reason to be cruel or unkind to anyone, Ever.

We are all here to Help each other in our Journey Through Life.

We can learn from each person.

Though we may disregard much of what someone is saying

If we do not agree with them, it is No reason to treat them or

Anyone else without Respect, Empathy and Gratitude.

Helping each other Selflessly, with no expectations, is the reason for

our Existence.

Be Kind to everyone, always and perhaps, we may be able to foster

A change in Consciousness altering the course of our future,

Leaving our Children a world that is Kind, Caring, Compassionate

and Loving.

Our Children's Legacy

The older generations, all hopeful when they were young, Failed.

Their failure is allowing our children to grow up in a

World of Fear, Greed, Prejudice, Inequality, Hatred, Hunger,

Homelessness, Climate Change, War and Distrust.

Instead of Helping Each Other, as Life is Meant to be Lived,

They focused only on their Survival and Success.

To change this paradigm, to make this world safer for our Children

to

Grow up in, it will take a Darwinian Shift of Consciousness,

Embracing Love over Fear, considering what is best for Everyone

Rather than only for Ourselves.

The Illusion of Happiness

There are two ways to view Happiness. One is what we Learned it to be.

We were taught Happiness comes from making a lot of money,

Having a house, car, family, doing things that will make You happy.

This type of happiness is an Illusion of Happiness,

As we Accept what we were Taught Happiness is.

The other type of Happiness comes from Within, from our Spirit.

This kind of Happiness results from doing things

Selflessly benefiting others, bringing Happiness to Everyone.

This type of happiness brings Inner Peace,

Including an understanding of the Meaning of Life.

Our Search for Meaning

When we begin to search for Meaning in Our Life

Questioning the truth of all we were taught,

We begin to Awaken and start the arduous journey

On the path towards Enlightenment.

This journey is long, often lonely, and quite challenging.

Only a few will reach the end of the path.

The journey often is not a choice for those who pursue it.

There is a gnawing unrelenting feeling Within no longer able to be

ignored.

This feeling comes from the Spirit, questioning all the choices and

Everything we had been taught and Accepted as true throughout our

life.

At this moment, we Awaken.

From this moment forward, your life will be changed forever.

You begin to question the friendships, job, marriage, and

Everything in your life as you embark on this new journey with

Those continuing to Live in an unenlightened world.

Surviving Is Not Enough

The Ego, which is everything we Learn and Accept as true

After we are born, allows us to survive in the world.

The Spirit, an Ethereal presence Within every life, however, gives

value

To our lives and allows us to embrace life more fully.

Though the Ego will always be an important part of our life,

To help us navigate and get by in the world,

It is the Spirit That Gives Our Lives Meaning.

On an Enlightened level, the Purpose of Life

Is to realize and Accept this, and by doing so, allow the

Unconditional Love of the Spirit, to be shared selflessly with all.

Spirituality vs Religion

Spirituality is quite different from Religion.

Religion is created by man.

It may have had good intentions when it began,

But Learned beliefs and intentions are False.

Spirituality comes from Within, where the Inherent beliefs of

God/Spirit/Soul, or whatever you may call it, exists.

These are the Pure Whole Emotions we were Meant to Share and

Live By.

Whereas Religion divides us, Spirituality joins us

Together to improve the life of all.

Have We Lived Our Lives in Vain?

We knew the answers when we were young.

We had the best music ever recorded. We were going to change the world.

Every generation feels this way. What happened?

The answer is Life.

Many of us got married, had families, bought a house,

Had bills, got a job, and Forgot. We settled into a life of mediocrity.

Eventually, we bought the Illusion of Happiness we Learned as we were growing up.

We began looking for answers in the world around us,

Rather than from Within, where we once knew the answers lie.

We failed.

The world Now is worse than when we were young.

Is it too late to change the world?

It is up to each of us to spread the message of

Unconditional Love, residing Within each of us, to all others.

To finish spreading the message we once knew to be true.

It is not too late to try to leave the world

A better place for our children.

If we do not, we all have lived our lives in vain.

Diew Life With Wonder and Awe

What is Learned during the first five years of a child's life,

May affect their Entire Life.

The many struggles we have throughout our lives often result from

the

Beliefs we developed during these early, impressionable years,

And the Acceptance of the many false self-centered egocentric

messages

We received as the truth, as we Learn our role in the world.

During these years if a child is taught to view the world and others

Through a Dark Negative Prism, one where Fear and concern for

yourself,

Dominate Love and concern for the well-being of Everyone,

The challenges these children will face will be great.

If, however, during these early years, they embrace Love Over Fear,

Concerned for the success and happiness of Everyone rather than only for themselves,

Their lives will take a much different direction.

These children will learn to understand the beauty of life, treat others and all life

With respect, and view life with Wonder and Awe, rather than Fear and Hate.

Love is All There Is

Why is there war, hate, fear?

Every unnecessary death is senseless, every negative emotion

harmful,

Not only to ourself, but to every life as well.

Open your heart, Listen.

What do you Hear, what do you Feel?

Love.

Everything else, everything we learned, every negative emotion,

Though accepted as normal throughout history must stop,

For our children and for the very survival of all life on our planet.

We Are All Related By a Common Purpose

We are all family, part of a greater spiritual universe

Related by a common purpose.

Every life, regardless of appearance, prestige, wealth

Or any other comparison we learned made us better than another

Is an important integral part of this universe

Equally deserving Respect, Happiness and Love.

What is the Meaning of Life?

In the 70's, I would have said The Meaning of Life

Was Sex, Drugs & Rock & Roll.

As I got older though, my definition changed.

The Meaning of Life is to begin to question if what we Learned,

And Accepted throughout our life was true (Awaken),

Realize and Accept Nothing we Learned (Ego) was True

(Enlightenment).

Sharing the Unconditional Love (Spirit)

(Love shared Selflessly, without expectation of getting anything in

return)

With All others, is the true Meaning of Life.

Finding Your Light

The answers we seek, to Find Your Light, enabling us to

Embrace Inner Peace, Love and Meaning in our Life,

May Never be found in the world by looking outside.

They may only be found by looking Within, where the Spirit exists.

Many of us intuitively understand this.

To Accept and Allow your Spirit to guide your

Journey Through Life, however, is quite challenging.

This is due to the dominance of the Ego (Self).

The Ego is everything we were Taught and Believe to be true since

our birth.

Awakening begins when we start to question everything we

Learned.

Enlightenment happens when we Accept as truth

Everything we learned was Wrong.

The journey is long, difficult, and often lonely.

The Meaning of Life is pursuing this journey,

Then Sharing Selflessly with all others your Light within.

Each of Us May Change the World

Jesus, Mohammed, Buddha and others called prophets throughout

history

Were simply human who fully embraced their Spirit Within,

Sharing the love residing there selflessly with all others.

The religions begun in their names have long ago lost their

Initial intention to help others realize this simple fact.

Each of us may choose to follow their path.

Doing so will not only bring Meaning to your life

But to all others who share your journey through life as well.

The Human Spirit

We are both Human (Ego) and the Essence Within (Spirit).

Our Human self is the cause of all man-made

Problems, hardships, and emotional stresses of humanity.

Our Essence (Spirit) is the shared calm, peaceful, loving sense

We feel when it is allowed to be part of our life.

Though both will always be present in our lives,

We have a choice which will be predominant.

Simply look at the world now and throughout history

To see the results of living in a Human world.

Perhaps it is time to consider the alternative,

One where Peace dominates War, Courage dominates Fear

And Love dominate Hate.

Do You Follow Your Heart or Your Mind?

When we primarily lead our life following our Heart (Spirit),

The beauty of the world reveals itself in numerous ways.

Love, present Within every life, is Shared to make life easier,

More meaningful for ourselves and others.

When we mostly follow the directions of our Mind (Ego), however,

Fear, learned when we are very young, dominates our life.

Fear is the cause of depression, anxiety, stress and also

Leads to all the unnecessary difficulties, hardships and struggles

Realized by so many throughout their lives.

Though both the Heart and Mind are necessary for our survival,

We each choose which path through life to mainly follow.

Choose to follow the more challenging path, the path of the Heart

(Love),

Opening our world to discovering Happiness and Meaning in our

lives,

Rather than the path we have always followed, the path of the Mind

(Fear),

Continuing us on a relentless downward spiral for

Both ourselves and our planet.

See the Soul Within

Every life has a Spirit.

Look into the eyes of another, to see the heart, soul, love existing

within.

This is true not only of people, but animals and all other forms of

life as well.

No one life is better or more important than another.

Embrace each other without conditions or judgment

To understand the reason we are born, the Meaning of Life.

I Am Confused

I did everything right.

I listened to my parents, teachers, went to church, did well in school,

Got a good education, a prestigious well-paying job, married, had

children,

Lived in a beautiful home filled with many expensive luxurious

items,

Ate at posh restaurants, took exotic vacations.

I had everything, yet I feel sad, lonely, empty.

My life lacks meaning. Why?

It is an illusion money, prestige, fame or anything else we

Learned will bring meaning or happiness in our life.

"It Will Not".

These must first be found Within, only then shared Selflessly with

all others.

Open Your Heart

When we are young we learn to protect ourselves from pain

Caused by others seeking to harm us with their words,

Deeds or actions, as they try to prove they are better than us.

We therefore live the rest of our life in Fear,

Afraid to reveal our true feelings and emotions to others.

Living in Fear, though we may be surrounded by many people,

Be successful, wealthy, famous, have many material possessions, we
will always

Be Alone, living a superficial life fearful of being hurt again.

It takes courage to Open Your Heart.

To truly understand and live a meaningful life, we must risk pain,

By sharing our Love within without reservation,

Understanding we no longer need to be protected

As we once were when we were young.

By challenging our childhood fears, we may finally be able to live

our

Life with Love rather than Fear, as we were always meant to.

It is How We Live That Has Meaning

Death is Inevitable.

It is how we live that gives our lives meaning.

Do we accept societies definition of success, becoming wealthy, famous,

Having a prestigious job (Ego) or anything else we Learned

Will allow us to live a worthwhile life, to decide if our life was meaningful?

Nothing We Learned in Life Will Bring Meaning.

True Meaning may only be found Within (Spirit) and will only be realized

When it is shared freely with all others.

Live in a World of Love

We have always lived in a world of chaos.

There has never been a time in history this has not been true.

There is no need to examine the results of living in such a world.

Simply study history and observe the world today

To see the reality of what living in such a world is like.

As more Awaken though, an alternative path becomes visible,

A path of Sharing, Hope and Empathy.

By embracing every life, ending hunger, homelessness, climate

change,

War and the many other man-made problems and inequities

We may finally be able to live in a World of Love instead.

Cherish Every Moment

Don't waste a single moment, squandering your brief existence

Chasing illusionary dreams we Learned will bring us success and

happiness.

"They Will Not".

Spend your life instead sharing your Essence and Love with all

others,

Making your life Meaningful and Important.

Our Purpose in Life

We are alive to discover and understand our purpose in life.

For most, the many diversions we each face every day

Make it difficult to appreciate the reason we are alive.

Though it may appear confusing, I assure you it is not.

We are alive to Embrace and Share our Love Within,

Helping others find their purpose in life as well.

Sadness

I am sad seeing a divided world where Fear, Hate,

Greed and Prejudice dominate the lives of so many.

Where concern for only ourself takes precedence

Over the survival of others and our planet.

It results in war, hunger, homelessness, climate change and

Almost all other problems experienced throughout time.

The technology exists Today to eliminate these

Negative feelings, emotions, and problems.

My sadness results from knowing this, realizing how few

Understand and are willing to change themselves and the world,

and

By doing so, helping everyone Live a Happy Meaningful life as

well.

Be Grateful For What You Have

If I knew then what I know now, I would have done many things differently.

I would have worked less, spent more quality time with my family and those I loved.

Not worried only about myself but tried to improve life for everyone.

Treated and respected all others as I would want to be.

Not been superficial, but rather sincere in all my interactions.

Been grateful for everything I had, not for those things I didn't have.

Shared my Love Selflessly with everyone, enjoyed the beauty and awe of life.

See the positive, rather than the negative in all others and in every encounter.

Understood the importance of the Spirit over the Ego.

Embraced life whole-heartedly, realizing the façade we disguise our true selves

With is the cause of much of our anxiety, stress, and unhappiness.

An Allegory of Life

We are like a grain of sand on a beach or a drop of water in an

ocean.

Part of a greater whole, without which the beach or ocean could not

exist.

It is only by merging all the sand and water

The splendor of the whole may be appreciated.

We are each like a grain of sand or drop of water.

Only Together may we all succeed, Learning the lessons we are here

to learn

And uncovering the reason we are alive.

The Mind, Body, Spirit Connection

Psychologists and Counselors enable us to return and function in

society,

But, often, their two-dimensional approach, treating

Only the Mind and Body, is deficient and inadequate.

Without also treating the Spiritual part of an illness, the treatment is

incomplete.

The Spirit gives our Lives Meaning.

Without also treating the Spirit, the result is simply a return to

mediocrity.

The constant internal struggle between the Mind and Body and the

Spirit,

Contributing to the symptoms of many illnesses and disorders,

Continues, allowing the illness to not be fully treated and return.

The Spirit Must therefore be included in

The treatment of many Psychiatric, as well as

Psychosomatic and Medical illnesses as well.

A Time for Change

We have the ability to feed the hungry, clothe and house the needy,

Provide fresh water to the thirsty, treat most illnesses,

End climate change, war, intolerance, and many other challenges

Now.

We must No longer accept these things as an irrefutable part of life.

It is time to alter this paradigm, ushering in a Spiritual Evolution,

Changing our dysfunctional world before it is too late,

For the survival and benefit of all life on our planet.

All Life is Sacred and Precious

Respect all life and Mother Earth.

Have empathy, be humble, truthful and considerate of everyone.

Only by caring and helping each other will all our lives

Become not only easier, but more Meaningful as well.

Together We Each Become Stronger

The Meaning of Life is not difficult to understand.

It is to share our Love Within with all living things.

By sharing this love Selflessly, each of us becomes stronger and

Our Journey Through Life less challenging and more Meaningful.

Believe

Believe the Messages you Hear Within.

They emanate from your Spirit/God/Soul residing inside Every Life.

These messages give our lives Meaning.

Following the guidance they provide will lead to Inner Peace, True Happiness,

Unconditional Love and a genuine understanding of Life's journey.

Ignoring this advice, Accepting everything we Learned and

Believed to be true (Ego), will lead instead to Conflict, Struggle,

Fear and all the many problems seen in the world.

We each choose our own path through life.

Perhaps it is time to Listen and Believe.

The Soul of Humanity

Though it may often appear humanity does not have a Soul,

As we observe many of the avoidable horrors and tragedies

We inflict on each other, we have simply forgotten.

Beneath the hatred, prejudice, desire for our Own success

Is a Spirit/Soul/God, representing Love,

Acceptance, and Hope for the success of Every life.

Humanity has always had a Soul, hidden within each life,

Waiting to be Rediscovered to usher in a new era of Peace and Love

for all.

Truth Lies Within

Awakening begins with gnawing doubts Emanating from Within

Questioning the validity of everything we have been Taught

And Accepted to be true since our birth.

Enlightenment occurs with the realization and Acceptance

everything

We have Learned in our life, that we had accepted as true, was Not.

Truth Lies Within. It may Never be found elsewhere.

When We Were Young

When We Were Young we Learned to be nice to others,

Treat everyone equally, be empathetic, loving and

Care about even those who were different from us.

As we got older, though, our definitions began to change.

We began to Accept society's Learned definitions of these emotions.

Just as with Religion and many other noble attempts to guide our

young and others,

Slowly we began to view each of these positive qualities through a

Self-Centered prism

Concerned now, how loving, being empathetic and caring for others

Benefited Us.

Instead of Unconditionally sharing our Love and viewing everyone

equally,

As we were taught when we were young through the Selfless lens of

the Spirit,

We began to accept Society's Self-ish, Egoistic view of the world

Being distorted by its Self-Centered view of life.

Perhaps, it is Not too late to change the world and give our children

A chance to experience life, as it was meant to be lived.

By all of us returning to the Pure, Genuine, Caring values

We first learned When We Were Young.

The Two Paths of Life

There are Two paths in life you may follow.

The path of the Ego or that of the Spirit.

Though the Ego will always remain with you throughout your life

To help you survive in the world, it does Not have to dictate your

choices.

It is when you allow your Spirit to predominantly influence

Your path through life, relegating the Ego to a secondary role,

Your life will truly become Meaningful.

What is Important in Life?

The time you have left as you approach death is an interesting time
in your life.

Many things, once appearing to be important, no longer are.

You begin to realize life really is not complicated or complex.

Rather, it is quite simple.

The money, material possessions, job you had, and almost
everything else you

Once thought defined what a "successful" life is, no longer matter.

Nothing will accompany you when you die.

You finally realize none of those things are important or ever were.

Don't wait until the end of your life to decide what is truly
important.

Live each day as if it was your last.

To discover what is important, close your eyes,

Relax your mind and body and Listen to the quiet voice Within.

Follow the suggestions you Hear (From your Spirit Guide),

Accepting its advice whole-heartedly, living the rest of your life

Selflessly helping others in their journey through life.

By doing so, when you near death, you will have no regrets

Having led a Meaningful life,

One full of True Love, Inner Peace and Happiness.

Follow the Spiritual Path

We each choose our direction through life, following either the

Learned path or deciding to pursue the Spiritual Path instead.

Accepting all we are Taught and Believed is true, abiding by

The status quo, Fearful of challenging the dictates of society,

Leads to a life riddled with doubt, anxiety, and mediocrity.

The Journey Through Life, however, is Not predestined.

We may instead choose to venture off the Accepted path in life

Detouring Inward, merging with our Spiritual Higher Self, leading

to

Love, Inner Peace, and a genuine understanding of the true Meaning

of Life.

Spirituality – Finding the Answers We Seek

Many seek answers in the many different religions

Created by man, though will Not find them there.

These religions long ago lost their significance and Meaning,

As they adopted Man's interpretation of right and wrong,

Good and evil, and other man-made comparisons.

There is another path, however, for those seeking Answers.

Spirituality is the belief there is a small piece of God (a Spirit or

Soul)

Within each life, and therefore Every life is Sacred,

Deserving to be treated with unconditional Respect and Love.

Spirituality is Innate, existing Within Every Life.

With the Acceptance of Spirituality comes Wisdom, Compassion,

Kindness, and Love for all Life.

Embracing Spirituality, will bring the Answers we seek as well as

Peace and Meaning to our lives.

Which Truth Will We Teach Our Children?

As we are Socializing our Children, especially early in their lives,

It is important to always be truthful and honest with them.

The question we each must ask ourselves is: What is the Truth?

To simplify this discussion, assume there are only two types of truth.

The first type of truth teaches our children to Accept the beliefs of

the world

As they are now and have been for millennia.

This truth emphasizes the individual, on what is Best for

Themselves,

Accepting the idea of living in a world of competition and distrust,

Being concerned only for their survival and happiness.

The other type of truth, however, has a very different view of life.

This truth emphasizes the collective, on what is Best for Everyone,

Accepting the idea of cooperation and trust, Selflessly Helping each other so

Everyone may Succeed in their Journey Through Life.

Most of the problems seen in the world result from living in an

Egocentric world concerned only for what is best for Ourselves.

All previous generations eventually have embraced this type of world.

It is a world of Fear, Hatred, Prejudice, Poverty, Homelessness,

Climate Change, Hunger, War, Cynicism, ad infinitum,

That will await our Children when they grow up.

We may only change this preordained future, by raising

The latest generation of children to be Selfless,

Unconditionally Sharing their Love Within with all others,

Assuring Everyone's survival and success in life.

One truth will lead to Struggle, To maintaining the status quo.

The other truth will lead to Enlightenment.

The only question we each must ask ourselves is:

Which Truth Will We Teach Our Children?

Memories

Good Memories enrich our lives of wonderful times gone by.

They often bring a smile on our face as we remember the past

When life was fun and we were happy.

There are also Bad Memories as well though, haunting our dreams and actions,

Often happening when something triggers a past event.

These Memories remind us of the many challenges we faced

As we struggled to survive and endure in an often-uncaring world.

These memories were both formed living in a world of uncertainty

And though the good memories may bring us happiness temporarily,

This happiness does not last, as the many daily struggles

We experience every day engulf us once more in life's daily challenges.

There is a third type of Memory though, often not considered.

This type of Memory is Inherent, present already in each of our cells,

In our DNA, when we are first born.

This Memory is found in Every Life throughout the universe,

Emanating from the Spirit Within.

Remembering and Sharing the Message of Unconditional Love

residing Within,

The Spirit gives Each Life Meaning and is the Reason we are born.

Unlike the brief feelings we experience with the other two types of

Memories,

Embracing the Inherent Spiritual Memories Within

Will bring Lasting Joy and Insight to our lives.

Sharing these Memories without Reserve with all others

Will also bring Inner Peace, Enduring Happiness, and a

True Understanding of the Meaning of Life.

Finding Happiness

We all wish to instill positive values in our children.

When our child is first born, we are Hopeful and Idealistic.

Being Caring, Respectful, Empathetic, Concerned for Others,

Accepting the importance of every life, are just a few of the positive

Beliefs

We encourage our children to Learn when they are young.

How we raise our children, especially when they are very young,

As they are Socialized, Taught and Learn how to survive in the

world,

Often determines if they will find Happiness during their life.

If our children are Taught to Accept the Beliefs in the world,

Being concerned primarily for what is Best for Themselves,

Rather than the Positive values we first hoped they would learn

When they were first born, though they may be Successful, become

famous,

Wealthy, have many material possessions, Are they truly Happy?

If, however, we raise our children to genuinely Accept and

Embrace the values we had hoped to share with them when they

were young,

When they were first born, and we were still Idealistic, perhaps they

will not

Need to struggle to find Happiness, inherently understanding

Happiness

Does not come from anything found in the world.

It only may be found Within, by Sharing the selfless positive values

Our parents once hoped we would Embrace when we were first

born.

We are All Ohana

Ohana means family in the Hawaiian language.

Here, family not only includes close relatives, but also, friends, neighbors,

And others (strangers) helping each other Selflessly.

Imagine living in a world of Ohana, one where Everyone

Supported and Cared about each other in times of need.

It is possible to live in such a world.

To do so we must discard our Learned Accepted beliefs of family,

Instead, Embracing and Helping each other regardless of

Any differences, with Open Arms and Unconditional Love.

To Change the paradigm of life, to improve the world for our Children,

Leaving them a planet where they can thrive, find happiness and meaning,

We must recognize we are all Ohana.

Only by Unselfishly Helping Each Other will we all Succeed.

And by doing so, discover the true Meaning of Life.

Sit Quietly and Listen

Who/What is God?

Religions throughout time have depicted God many ways.

Though Religion may have had good intentions when it began,

It quickly deteriorated into defining God using Learned words and

practices.

Doing this, Religion ended up Dividing

Rather than Uniting us as it was first meant to do.

There is another definition of God, however, that must be

considered.

God/Spirit/Soul, it does Not matter what it is called,

Is an Ethereal Spiritual entity Within every life,

Accompanying each being in its Journey Through Life.

To understand the Meaning of Life, Sit Quietly and Listen.

Sharing your Light with the World

It is much easier to Accept the status quo, recognizing the many

problems

Experienced by many as inevitable, having little recourse to help

others.

Look at the world today and throughout history

To see what Living in such a world is like.

It is a world of Fear, Hate, Prejudice, War, Hunger,

Homelessness, Climate Change, ad infinitum.

Every person Can change the world.

We each have, Within us, the Means to do so.

It begins by Listening quietly, Accepting the messages you Hear

Then Sharing your Light with the World.

How to Find Meaning in Your Life?

The Meaning of Life may be found by destroying the barriers

We artificially erect, from Learning, Believing and Accepting

All we were Taught during our life.

Inner Peace, Happiness and Meaning in Life will

Only be found by unselfishly Sharing the hidden Love,

Present Within every life, with all others.

Listen

All we must do to Awaken, Become Enlightened and

Find Inner Peace and Happiness,

Is sit in a comfortable chair,

Close our eyes,

Quiet our mind and

Listen.

The Cause of Loneliness

How can someone, surrounded by people, at home,

Work, on the streets be totally alone?

If all others see is the artificial facade we learned to project

When we were young children, even those closest to us,

Our family, may not be able to penetrate this barrier (Ego).

We therefore go through life completely alone,

Struggling every day, desperately trying to find Friendships,

Intimacy, and Love.

To break through the façade, open your heart, Share your Love

Within

With others allowing your Authentic self (Spirit) to shine its Light,

Ending your loneliness and by doing so, bring Meaning,

Companionship, and Love to your life.

We Are One

Every Life is Valuable, Equal and Connected,

Linked together, having a Spirit/Soul/God Within,

Helping guide each of us with Love, Knowledge and Purpose.

Always show Respect, Helping each other selflessly, despite the

many

Petty Learned differences we are brought up to Believe are

important.

"They Are Not".

We are all Related, linked together by a Shared Intent to Support

each other,

So we all may equally Succeed, Flourish and Find Meaning in our

Life.

Do Not Waste Your Life Living in Fear

If we measure time from the beginning of the universe

Our Life passes like a grain of sand on a beach or a drop of water in

an ocean.

To waste our insignificant life living in Fear, Believing we are

Better than another, Accepting the Lies we have been taught

About Our Importance in the World, Masks the purpose of Life.

We Each decide what our Journey Through Life will be.

To live a Meaningful Life, in the time we are alive,

Ignore everything you have been Taught and Accepted

As genuine about your Importance in the World.

Accepting you are Not that significant.

Every life is Equally Important.

Unlimited Possibilities

I Am Asleep when I Accept the world as it is

Believing there is nothing I can do to help others

Or change the many atrocities and inequalities affecting so many.

I begin to Wake (Awaken) from my slumber when I question my

apathy.

I fully Wake Up (Enlightenment) when I open my eyes

Seeing the unlimited possibilities life has to offer,

Realizing there is much I can do to improve the future for everyone.

Our Hope for Change

Every generation hopes to bring change.

Yet, after millennia, we live in a cruel, often unforgiving world

Continuing to Ignore the needs of the Many, instead seeking

Only our own Self-ish desires and pleasures.

The numerous problems seen throughout the World,

Climate Change, Hunger, Homelessness, Extreme Poverty, ad

infinitum,

Are caused by Fear, Greed, Hate, and Prejudice,

Instilled in each of us as we were Socialized to believe the Big Lie.

This Lie taught us to Accept and Inflate Our importance

In the World over the Importance of all others.

Only when we all Succeed, Sharing the resources on this planet

Equally,

May the paradigm of life be altered allowing the Fear, Greed, Hate

and

Prejudice to fade away, bringing the Change Each Generation

Had so desperately hoped for.

The Eyes You See the World Through

Look at the world.

Do you see clear crisp colors, undiluted by the challenges

experienced by so many?

Do you see an uncaring world in disarray or a world of endless

possibilities?

How you view the world and others depend on the eyes you see it

through.

If you accept all you were taught, the world will indeed be a dark

place,

Its shaded colors muted by an array of impure hues.

If, however, the world is seen through your Spirit/Soul Within

Your vision will become clear revealing the unlimited potential of

life.

The Spiritual Path

Enlightenment is a journey, often long, challenging, and lonely,

Many Have No Choice but to follow.

Despite how Successful our life may be,

There is a feeling deep Within, something is wrong.

A feeling that simply will not abate.

This Awakening, will lead to disavowing Everything

We have Learned and Accepted as True during our lifetime.

Beginning us on a Spiritual Path of Self-Discovery.

Living in a Competitive World

Many of the problems and illnesses around the planet

Result from Living in a Competitive World.

It is a World where concern is focused only on Our survival,

On what is best for Us, rather than the Survival and what is best for

Everyone.

From the moment of our birth, we are Taught to

Embrace this False Path through life.

With Awakening, we begin to question if this Learned egocentric path

Is wrong and is the reason for the uneasy Feeling Within,

Wondering if there may be More to Life.

Enlightenment results as we finally Accept Everything we

Were Taught and Learned was true, Was Not.

At this point, we understand The Meaning of Life

Is to Equally Share Everything with all others, allowing

Everyone to be Happy and Live a Successful Life as well.

We are Not Alone

We are all here to help each other on our Journey Through Life.

Reach out when you are down.

We will help pick you up and gently guide you

To the path you are meant to follow.

This is what we were always meant to do,

To truly care about each other, helping each other Selflessly.

By Sharing our Love with others,

Our lives will be Meaningful and an Inner Peace

Will replace the Chaos dwelling Within.

Which Future Will We Choose?

Why is there hunger, homelessness, hate, fear?

Why is there prejudice, poverty, inequality, war?

These are only a few of the emotions and actions of a dying species,

One where their children will perish in a soon to be uninhabitable

land.

It is Not too late to stop this future, though time for change is rapidly

passing.

Embrace each other and the Spiritual message Within, open your

heart

To living in a world of Love rather than Hate ensuring a bright

future

For our children and the planet we all share together.

The First Step in Your Spiritual Journey

Everything you Learn and Accept as real since you were born is

untrue.

Understanding this is the first step in your Journey towards

Spirituality.

We are socialized to believe Our Happiness and Meaning

Result from our Actions and Success in the world.

Nothing could be further from the truth.

The Truth may Never be found in the World.

It may only come from Within.

If you Listen silently all the answers you seek, will reveal

themselves

To you and the Lesson you are here to learn will finally be realized.

Within

Within everything alive there is an Essence.

Whether you call this Essence Spirit/Soul/God

Or anything else, it does not matter.

It is an Ethereal presence connecting all life together,

Giving our lives Meaning.

Awakening happens when we first sense this presence

Is truly there and may be important in our life.

Enlightenment is reached when we Accept it is more important

Then the Ego, which encompasses everything we have

Learned and Believed to be True since we were born.

We finally understand the value of Every life, not just Our own life,

As the Meaning of Life finally becomes clear.

What if I Die Today?

Life is very uncertain and unpredictable.

Despite our health and age, any of us could die today.

Your wealth, race, sex, or any other comparison may not save you

from death this day.

There is much uncertainty what happens after we die.

Many hope there is More after Death.

Until the moment after we die, though, we will never truly know.

Would we approach life differently if we knew death was

Imminent?

Those who are gravely ill, knowing they will die soon,

Often review their life when death is approaching,

Realizing there is much they wish they had done differently.

When this moment happens, almost all have regrets.

Money, Material Possession, Fame, and anything else we thought

Would make our lives Successful, suddenly are Meaningless.

On the day we will die, we finally understand our

Priorities in life were wrong. We Wasted our life.

We had lived our life in Fear, Accepting the Self-Centered

Egoistic path through life we were Taught

Would allow us to lead a "successful" life.

On that day, we finally understand what was truly important.

We realize, to lead an Important Meaningful life we must Open our

Heart,

Sharing the Love Within Selflessly not only with those closest to us,

But with all others as well. Approach life as if you will die today.

Live Every Day with Love, instead of Fear by Opening Your Heart.

If you do, on the day you will die, you will have No Regrets,

Having had the chance to Make a Difference,

By Sharing your Love while you were still alive.

For on that day just Before you die you will realize

Your life was Worthwhile and Meaningful.

We Can Change the World

When we were young, it was the greatest of times.

We believed we would change the world, but did we?

If we look at the world today, the answer most certainly must be No.

We fell into a pattern so many generations do.

Trying to survive in the world, we forgot the importance of

Caring about each other Selflessly.

We eventually Accepted society's egocentric definition of Success

and Happiness.

It is Not too late, though, to open our hearts and share

Our Love unconditionally with all others.

By doing so, we can change the direction of the world, helping

Everyone Succeed,

Leaving the world a better place for our children and each other.

Embrace Life

If you live your life with Fear, worried about Your Survival and

what is

Best for You, every day you Fear both Life and Death.

If, however, you live your life with Love,

You fear Neither, freeing you to Embrace Life to its Fullest,

Making your life Meaningful by Sharing

Your Love Selflessly with all others.

Will We Choose War or Peace?

There has never been a millennia where there has been peace.

War, Hate, Prejudice, Greed, Fear have always dominated our lives

(Ego).

As long as our focus is isolated on ourselves, on what is best for Us

And not on what is best for others and our planet, nothing will

change.

Life will continue as it has, until the earth becomes barren.

The only way to stop this inevitable cycle towards extinction is to

embrace Peace.

Not the temporary peace we learned about when there is no war,

But the peace found Within every life (Spirit).

With the Acceptance of the Spiritual path true Happiness,

Meaning and Tranquility surround your very being.

To change the future and the destructive path our planet is on,

We must adopt this type of Peace, Sharing its message with others,

Giving our children a chance to grow up in a

World of Peace and Love rather than War and Hate.

Our Education

After we are born, our Education begins.

The Illusion of Happiness occurs when we look for our happiness

By doing all the thing we Learned, Accepted and Believed

Will make us happy as we were growing up.

"They Will Not".

To find true Happiness, Spiritually, Share the Light and Love

Within

Each of us Selflessly helping all others find their Light as well.

What is Freedom?

We share our planet with many others.

Not only people, but animals, plants, and other forms of life as well.

Yet we treat each other and our planet as being insignificant and

unimportant.

Many are so concerned about their freedom they simply ignore

All others, concerned only for what is Best for themself.

By doing so, we are not only alienating ourselves from each other

But from doing what is best for all life on our planet and

Even for the survival of our planet itself.

Unless we change our definition of Freedom to include treating

All Life and the Earth with equal respect

Caring for what is Best for Everyone, not only Ourselves

The downward spiral of life will continue unabated,

Leaving our children to be raised in an unsustainable world of Fear

and Hate.

Freedom is equally respecting and treating all life and each other

As we Ourselves wish to be treated.

It is time for each of us to decide: What is Freedom?

Is this the World We Want for our Children?

We live in a World of Malice and Division, judging others due their

differences.

Race, Religion, Sex, Sexual Orientation, Wealth, Fame

Among many other distinctions, divide rather than unite us.

Those who are Poor, Old, Disabled, Homeless, Work Menial Jobs,

Lack education or any other trait defining failure by society are

treated

As Second Class Citizens, unworthy of being Helped or Cared

About.

Is this the World we wish for our Children?

If it is, nothing needs to be done. We are doing an Excellent Job.

If, however, We Want More for our Children, leaving Them a

World of Hope,

A world where we Help and Care about each other regardless

Of Any Differences among Us, Change Must begin Now.

It is up to Each One of Us to usher in this Change before it is too
Late.

How Life is Meant to be Lived

All who are struggling, for whatever reason, must be recognized,

helped, and cared for.

All our resources should be equally shared.

There should Not be hunger, homelessness, climate change, War,

Poverty,

Religious Conflict, Discrimination, or any of the many other

Isolating afflictions plaguing the World.

We can rid ourselves of these problems Now.

All we lack is the Will to do so.

Helping each other is how life is meant to be lived.

Only then may our hearts soften allowing us to understand

The true reason we are alive and the Meaning of Life.

Our Light

When we are born, our Light (Spirit) shines brightly.

With each passing day, though, as we Learn, Accept and

Believe what we are Taught (Ego), our Light begins to dim.

As we get older, we may begin to question the truth of what we were

Taught,

Hoping to rediscover our bright Light within (Awaken).

If we are successful, Accepting everything we Learned

During our life from the Ego is the cause of our darkening radiance,

Our Light will once again Shine brightly

As it was always meant to do (Enlightenment).

Always Do Right

In every situation, there is Never cause to harm another.

It does not matter if the injury is physical, verbal, taking

Advantage of another, or any other reason.

Treating all others with Love, Respect and Empathy

Is Always the right thing to do.

Challenge Everything You Are Taught

We spend our life undoing the Damage done as we are Taught how

We should act and what we should Believe as we are growing up

(Ego).

Though these things are necessary to survive in the world

They end up dominating our lives instead of being an aid

To our survival, as they were meant to be.

To undo the damage, challenge everything you were Taught,

Embracing the

Message Within as your primary guide through life instead (Spirit).

We Are Imperfect

With our birth our imperfection begins as we are exposed to the

many lies

We are Taught will bring Happiness and Meaning to our lives.

Nothing we Learn will do that.

Instead, what we learn leads to the unnecessary hardships and

imperfections many face.

Not only the numerous problems and inequalities observed

throughout the world

But also, the many inner demons and anxieties we experience as

well.

We often spend our entire life chasing a dream we were Taught was

true.

"It Never Was".

To rid ourselves of our imperfections, to find true happiness and

Meaning in your life, open your heart, Listen

Changing the direction of your life by Accepting the message you hear.

An Inflection Point

War or Peace, Hate or Love, Fear or Courage

Selfishness (Caring only about ourself) or

Selflessness (Caring equally for all).

Will we continue to follow our Ego, Accepting all the false things

We were taught and Accepted as true or our Spirit,

Accepting its message Within of Peace, Love, Courage and

Selflessness?

More than any time in history we must choose now.

There is No more time for pause.

One path leads to Extinction, the other to Evolution.

Are We Really Different?

Though we each are unique in appearance, personality, beliefs,

Success, prestige and in so many other ways, we are all the same,

Alive, part of a collective of many with a unifying common purpose,

To share our Spiritual Love Within creating a world of

Peace, Equality, and Harmony.

Happiness, Love and Meaning

We all, on our journey through life, seek Happiness, Love and

Meaning.

Whether these wonderful attributes are found, however,

Depend on where you are seeking them.

Though many, having achieved success during their life,

Having wealth, a home, family, and many material possessions,

Believe they found Happiness, Love and Meaning,

They have simply bought into the Illusion, the Learned myth these

things

May be bought or found in the world.

"They Cannot".

In truth, Happiness, Love and Meaning must First be found Within

each of us

And then, will only be realized, by Sharing it Selflessly with all

others.

Becoming One With Our Higher-Self

A small piece of God (Spirit), representing Peace, Love and Light,

Reside Within all living things, including people, animals,

Plants, and even the universe itself.

Becoming One with God (our Higher-Self), Sharing its message of

Love with all life

Selflessly is the simple lesson we are here to learn.

Help Each Other

Listen, Hear, Share.

Listen to the soft whispers within.

Hear its message of Love.

Share your Love freely with All.

It is everyone's responsibility to Help each other,

Allowing each to succeed in their Journey Through Life.

The Answers in Life

Many hope to find Answers in their life.

They search for them through religion, hoping to find God and

Meaning there.

Though when religions first began they attempted

To help others discover spirituality, they soon became corrupted,

As human interpretations were given to the most basic tenets being

taught.

They also searched for answers by attempting to "succeed" in the

world,

Making a lot of money, having many material possessions (Ego).

Yet, despite being religious and wealthy, the answers to life they

Were seeking, the inner peace, happiness and love could not be

found.

The answers to life may "only" be found Within (Spirit),

Where they have always been.

They must "first" be found there, then shared without intention with the world.

Close Your Eyes

All we have to do to Awaken,

Become Enlightened and

Find Inner Peace and Happiness,

Is sit in a comfortable chair,

Close your eyes,

Quiet your mind, and

Listen.

The Seeker

We spend our entire life seeking, looking for

Happiness, Answers, Meaning in our life.

We search for these throughout the world, adopting religion,

Making money, buying material possessions, having a family,

prestigious job

Or any of the many other things we Learned would aid in our quest

(Ego).

Despite our efforts, what we seek will Never be found in our

lifetime.

Though we may have led a successful life, obtained the very best life

Has to offer, what we seek may not be found in the World.

It may only be found Within every life (Spirit), where the answers

we have

Sought our entire life, searching endlessly in the world, have always

been.

A Spiritual Evolution

Our thinking is dictated by the Ego, what we Learned and Accepted

As true as we were indoctrinated and Socialized

To Believe societies traditions, mores, and customs.

Nothing will change if we continue to follow this path through life.

Only when our Thinking, Beliefs and Actions are dictated

By our Spirit, Within, may true change finally happen,

Leading to a Spiritual Evolution on our planet.

We All Need Love

Everything Alive Needs Love.

Not just people, but animals and all other life as well.

The Love I am talking about isn't Learned and Conditional.

It is Inherent, coming from Within, given Selflessly and

Wholeheartedly without concern of receiving anything in return.

Sharing our Love with others not only brings

Meaning to our Life but to all others as well.

Understanding and Accepting this is why we are alive.

It is the Lesson we are here to Learn.

Is Your Life More Important Than Another's?

Be Considerate of Everyone.

Your Decisions should Always be made

Considering Others, not only Yourself.

Though there may be many differences between us,

Your Life is Not more important than Another's.

To Change the World

It is important to begin with our children.

Teaching them to live their lives with Love rather than Hate,

Curiosity rather than Fear, Acceptance rather than Prejudice,

Selflessness rather than Selfishness.

If the next generation of children are brought up this way,

Then perhaps it may not be too late

To change our destiny and our future.

The Alternative Is Unthinkable

We live in an extremely egocentric dysfunctional world.

It will take a Shift of Consciousness to bring change.

If we do not begin to make this change Now, our little speck of light

In the universe will soon cease to be able to support life.

All of us must help.

Once you wake up from your slumber, it is important to Share

With others the wisdom you gleaned to Help our planet Evolve.

The Alternative Is Unthinkable.

Will Life on Earth be Missed Once it is Gone?

There are 100 billion galaxies in the known universe,

Each one containing billions upon billions of stars.

Each one of those stars may have multiple planets in orbit around them.

There, therefore, are trillions of planets in the universe.

Will life on earth be missed once it is gone?

No.

Life will continue undeterred elsewhere in the universe.

Our destruction, all but assured, if we continue following the egoistic path

We have always pursued will barely cause a tiny ripple in space.

There is very little time left to change this preordained future.

Only be Embracing each other, helping cure the world of its many

Man-made destructive ways, will life on Earth and the Earth itself heal,

Allowing our children a chance to meet and join the many other

Sentient forms of life present throughout the galaxies.

What is Best for Everyone?

When we consider the many man-made divisions seen throughout

the world,

Whether it be our different Political, Religious, Tribal or any other

differences

Determined by our Socialization, the Only question we must ask

Ourselves is

What is Best for Everyone?

Living in an Egocentric World, where we only ask What is Best for

Me,

Is the cause of all the Hate, Fear, Prejudice, Wars, Hunger,

Homelessness,

Climate Change and many of the other problems existing

In the world today and throughout History.

If we Only considered what is Best for Everyone we would equally

Share our Resources ridding the world of Hunger and

Homelessness.

Treat Each person with Respect, Love and Empathy, regardless of

Their Differences, to rid the world of Fear, Hate and Prejudice.

Making the World a Kinder, more Caring Home for all.

Living in a Spiritual World

Living in a spiritual world war, fear, hatred and all other negative

Emotions and man-made challenges would not exist.

Peace would reign as greed and egocentric worries

Would give release to Love and Empathy for all.

Close your eyes, Listen quietly, Hear the message within and

Choose to live in this world now.

The Absurdity of War

Senseless death to benefit and enrich the few leading to the

Extinction of so many for absolutely no discernible reason.

Instead of helping and caring for others, we choose to extinguish

their Light.

There is Never a reason to accept this absurdity.

Life is far too precious to allow pointless death.

We Must reject the myth war is an inevitable necessary part of life,

Embracing instead Peace, Love and Hope, allowing for the Spiritual

evolution

Of our planet, assuring a future for our children and all others.

We Are All on the Same Journey Through Life

Every life is valuable, important, deserving

To be treated with Dignity, Love and Empathy.

Nothing we Learned makes us different from each other.

Though we may look and act different, believe differently about

religion,

Have more money, prestigious job, material possessions

Or any number of other things that differentiate us from one another,

That Matters Little.

Those who remain asleep, Believe and Accept what they were

Taught

And Observed, Believing we are truly different, better than others

(Ego).

We are all on the Same Journey Through Life.

Only by helping and treating each other with respect and love,

As we each hope to be treated ourselves, will we all flourish and

Live a truly successful meaningful life (Spirit).

We Are All Connected

We live in a world worrying about Ourselves, Our Happiness and

Existence.

Accepting this path through life, we are Alone

Surrounded by a sea of people, separated from each other,

Struggling to Survive, isolated in a world of injustice and inequalities,

Passively accepting the horrors and disparities living in such a world

brings.

It need not be this way.

We are All Connected. We are All One.

Within every living thing, a Spirit is present

Connecting each of us, each life, to each other.

By Embracing our common connection, helping others

Everyone may Succeed in life.

Doing this, may finally change the paradigm of life,

Bringing True Happiness and Meaning to all our Lives.

There is Never a Reason to Hurt Another

Regardless of the slight or pain caused every life deserves

To be treated with Respect, Empathy and Love.

We Learn we should get even with others if they hurt us.

We Must Not.

This fallacy results in feelings of inadequacy, stress,

Anxiety, depression as well as numerous other struggles

Experienced by so many throughout their life.

We are meant to Help, not Harm, each other.

To Embrace not Distance, Love not Hate, Be Courageous not

Fearful.

The path of Helping, Embracing, Loving and Being Courageous

Will lead to the Spiritual Evolution of our planet.

The current path on our planet, however, of causing

Harm, Distance, Hate and Fear

Will only lead to further misery, struggle and extinction.

It is up to each of us to determine our future.

By never hurting another, accepting each other,

Without conditions or judgment, we may finally change the

destructive

Trajectory of our planet allowing us to evolve as a species,

By accepting what is good Within each of us, rather than only what

is bad.

A Deeper Reason

We are each alive more than to just survive and Succeed in the

world (Ego).

There is a much deeper reason.

Only by understanding and accepting this,

Can the Illusion we were taught to believe be shattered.

Only by opening our Hearts and Helping each other,

Without expectation, so everyone can survive and

Be equally successful will we find true happiness

And Meaning in our Life (Spirit).

One With God

The Spirit, which represents a small piece of Essence (God),

Is present Within all living things and connects all life.

To become One with God (Our Higher-Self),

Emanating from Within every life, is our purpose, our meaning in

life.

By Sharing the inherent Love present there with all others,

Without expectation of benefit for ourselves, we amplify its power

Exponentially to improve all our lives.

With this realization, one Awakens and becomes Enlightened.

The Purest Form of Communication

To Awaken and become Enlightened is just the beginning of our

journey.

To be able to peer directly into the Soul (Spirit) of another is

The next logical step in the Spiritual growth and evolution of

humanity.

This is the purest form of communication.

Too often we judge others by their appearance, actions, and other

Factors influenced by society and our upbringing.

To be able to truly know someone, not as a product of who they

appear to be,

But rather as a pure Spirit, is how we are meant to see and relate

with each other.

We Are Immortal

Death is not the end. Rather it represents a new beginning.

The Spirit of the person or any life who died,

Though no longer physically here, will forever continue to live on in

The Heart and Spirit of those it met and influenced during its life.

It does not matter how brief the encounter is.

Every interaction we have with another will affect

Both your and their path through life.

As a result, both of your life journey's will forever

Be altered and our presence (Spirit) will be

Immortalized in their Heart forever.

The Dominance of the Spirit

Awakening is when there is a realization there is a Spirit within each

living thing.

Enlightenment is simply the Acceptance of this.

When one becomes Enlightened, though the Ego,

Which is everything we Learn and Believe to be true,

Will always remain with each of us throughout our lives,

It no longer dominates our thoughts and actions.

The Spirit now becomes our primary decision maker.

With Enlightenment comes wisdom,

Compassion, kindness, and love for every life.

Helping Each Other

We can change the world Today. We only lack the will to do so.

Technology exists Now to eliminate many Man-made scourges from

our planet.

The only thing preventing this is the greed and selfishness

Of those who consider wealth more important than people.

For this to happen, we must challenge everything we Learn and

Believe to be true

Throughout our life, renouncing the ideology of competition and

self-interest,

Replacing it with universal concern for every life in its stead.

In the wake of this monumental change, will lie a world where

There is Love, Empathy, and Compassion for everyone instead.

Where Our Spirit Exists

The answers to life, meaning and happiness,

May only be found within, where our Spirit exists.

They may Never be found elsewhere.

Only by sharing our love without expectation, not just with those

closest to us,

But with everyone else as well, will we find what we have always

searched for.

Happiness and meaning do Not come from all the things

We think they come from in the world.

Rather they will only be found from the unconditional Love

We share with each other.

Memories of the Past

Imagine a world where our children

Are raised to understand the Spirit within them.

They would be brought up knowing compassion,

Empathy, and the importance of treating everyone equally.

No longer would we ignore the suffering of others.

Rather, we would help all those in need, struggling through life's

many challenges.

Our children would be raised in a world where Love is Freely

Shared with all others for the betterment of all life and

Where hate, fear and greed are simply memories of the past.

Our Destiny

To fulfill our destiny,

We must be willing to confront and challenge our past.

To take a chance, changing the path we are on and the direction our

life is taking.

It is simply easier to continue as we always have,

Believing and Accepting everything we have been taught

To be true since we were born.

Continuing to allow life to happen to us,

Will only bring further misery and unhappiness.

Only by taking control of our life, will the answers and

Meaning in life finally become evident.

The Answers

The answers we seek must be First

Be found Within.

Only then may they be Shared Freely

And Selflessly with others.

Our Guide Within

We are All Related,

Linked together by a Shared Intent,

Having a Spirit/Soul/God Within,

Helping guide each of us with Love,

Universal Knowledge and Purpose.

Change

Every person can change the world.

We each have, Within us, the Means to do so.

It begins by Listening quietly,

Accepting the messages you Hear

Then Sharing your Light

With the World.

Our Journey of Rediscovery

We are all on the same journey of Rediscovery,

Trying to return to the Spiritual Path

We once knew when we were first born,

Rather than the Learned Socialized Path

We were Taught by the Ego.

Accept the Message You Hear

We Each Can Change the World

By Listening to the quiet voice Within,

Accepting its message,

Then Sharing it Selflessly

With all others.

Look Within Your Heart

Do not waste your entire life

Searching throughout the world for

What is already Within your Heart.

Author's Note

It is our hope your Journey Towards Enlightenment has been enhanced by reading "*Spiritual Reflections: A Book About Awakening and Enlightenment*". If it has, could you "*Please*" take a few minutes to:

"Write a Review"

and perhaps recommend this book on *Social Media* and to your *Friends and Family*. Bodhi and I wrote this book to try to *Awaken* and help others, who are *Awakened,* more fully understand what *Enlightenment* is, so their *Spiritual Journey Through Life* may be more fully realized.

Thank you for taking the time to read

"*Spiritual Reflections: A Book About Awakening and Enlightenment*"

Please spread our message, for we are all traveling life's journey together.

We hope you will also read all the books in "*The Awakening*

Tetralogy":

"Today I Am Going to Die: Choices in Life"

"The Spirit Guide: Journey Through Life"

"Tranquility: A Village of Hope"

"The Illusion of Happiness: Choosing Love Over Fear"

{Please check out my website: http://kenluball.com to learn more about these books}

Feel free to Share your Thoughts & Questions about "Spirituality" with me @: findingyourlight14@gmail.com

Let's share our *Journey Through Life* together. Please check out my **"Blog & Website"** and Follow/Like/Friend me on **"Facebook, Instagram, You Tube, Twitter, Pinterest, LinkedIn & Reddit".**

About Ken

Peace, Love & Light

****

My name is Ken Luball. Spiritual Seeker ~ Author ~ Guide

****

Author of "The Awakening Tetralogy: A Series of Four Spiritual Novels"

And Spiritual Reflections, a book of Spiritual Poetry

****

Ever since I was a young child, I knew my purpose in life; it was

for me to Awaken, find Enlightenment, and share my experience and

knowledge with others. To reach those lofty aspirations though, I first had to navigate through quite a few unexpected detours in my life. Though I was brought up in a religious family, it did not help me *Hear* the messages from my *Spirit Guide, Bodhi.* If anything, religion only further isolated me, teaching me to accept the *Ego's* view of religion rather than *Bodhi's.* It was not until after I stopped following a formal religion, I finally was able to embrace *Spirituality,* and with this embrace, I *Awoke.*

Spirituality is the belief there is a piece of God (a *Spirit*) within everything that has life, and, because of this, all life is important, equal, and connected. After I *Awoke,* no longer having the dogma of religion handicapping my views, I was suddenly free to explore this philosophy of life more deeply. Only then did I become aware of the *Mask* I wore and the impenetrable *Wall* I had erected around my Heart; the *Mask* and *Wall* allowed me to survive in the world. I would always smile, appear happy, though, I would often feel intense anxiety within. This was something I never really understood until the moment I confronted my *Ego.* Little did I know, these survival mechanisms would have a profound effect on me for the majority of my life. By protecting me from emotional pain, they also isolated me from my family, everyone else in my life, and even from myself. No one could hurt me because I did not allow anyone to get close enough to do so. In turn, no one could love me or was I able to truly love another either. This superficial life, one devoid of risk or pain, left me *alone* in a sea of people.

It took many years before the first cracks in my *Wall* formed and before I could loosen the *Mask* I constantly wore. It took me almost an entire lifetime to become to be *Awakened* and begin my journey towards *Enlightenment*.

After I was clearly able to *"hear"* my *Spirit Guide, Bodhi,* I realized everything I had *Learned* from my *Ego* throughout my life was untrue. I had looked for love and happiness in the job I had, the money I made, things I owned, and through my wife and children. With the exception of the latter, I finally realized none of those things truly mattered. This does not mean I am ungrateful to my *Ego,* however. It taught me coping skills and allowed me to "succeed", or at least what I was taught success was. Though my *Ego* still remains with me, it has taken a more secondary position in my life now, relinquishing its former primary role to *my Spirit Guide, Bodhi.*

Decisions were now required. While it was tempting to take this newly found state of being and withdraw from society and all the hate, fear, cruelty, poverty, and greed that plagues it, I knew within myself this gift of Enlightenment was to be shared with others. That is my destiny. Therefore, I have written "The Awakening Tetralogy", a series of four Spiritual books, and "Spiritual Reflections", a book of Spiritual poetry, to share this knowledge with as many others as possible. It is my and Bodhi's *hope you will read these books, and in doing so, begin a new adventure. One where you will* Awaken *and further your journey towards* Enlightenment *with your Spirit Within.*

I do not know if our books will be read widely in my lifetime, though I hope one day they may help others Awaken and find Enlightenment as well.

"We are all on a Spiritual Journey of Love & Peace; together may we spread "Light" throughout the world"

***

Ken Luball is a Spiritual Seeker ~ Author ~ Guide ~ on a mission to help Awaken as many people as possible. Born and raised in the US, Ken has had a lifelong obsession with finding the true Meaning of Life, and with his Spirit Guide, Bodhi, has successfully penned "*The Awakening Tetralogy*" and a book of poetry of stories, anecdotes, and lessons he has learned along the way. When he is not writing, Ken can be found enjoying 70's era classic rock and roll and folk music, hiking, interacting with his substantial social media following, and instilling the message of true joy into the hearts of his family and others.

To read more of Ken's life-changing reflections visit his Website: http://kenluball.com or reach out to him at findingyourlight14@gmail.com .

Appendix - List of Spiritual Reflections

Made in the USA
Middletown, DE
08 July 2022

68728155R10159